Try to make Moments that Matter! Hope you enjoy our book

Stan Smith

Hope our book encourages you to SERVE well!

Gary Niebur

STAN SMITH & GARY NIEBUR

WINNING TRUST

HOW TO CREATE MOMENTS THAT MATTER

WINNING TRUST
HOW TO CREATE MOMENTS THAT MATTER

COPYRIGHT© 2024 BY SMITH AND NIEBUR PUBLICATIONS, LLC

PUBLISHED AND DISTRIBUTED BY SMITH AND NIEBUR PUBLICATIONS, LLC

PRINTED IN CHINA

COVER DESIGN AND LAYOUT BY DAVID VALENTINE

ISBN: 979-8-218-42593-7

TO OUR WIVES
MARGIE AND TERESA,

TO OUR FAMILIES,

AND TO THE ENTIRE STAN SMITH EVENTS TEAM—
PAST, PRESENT, AND FUTURE

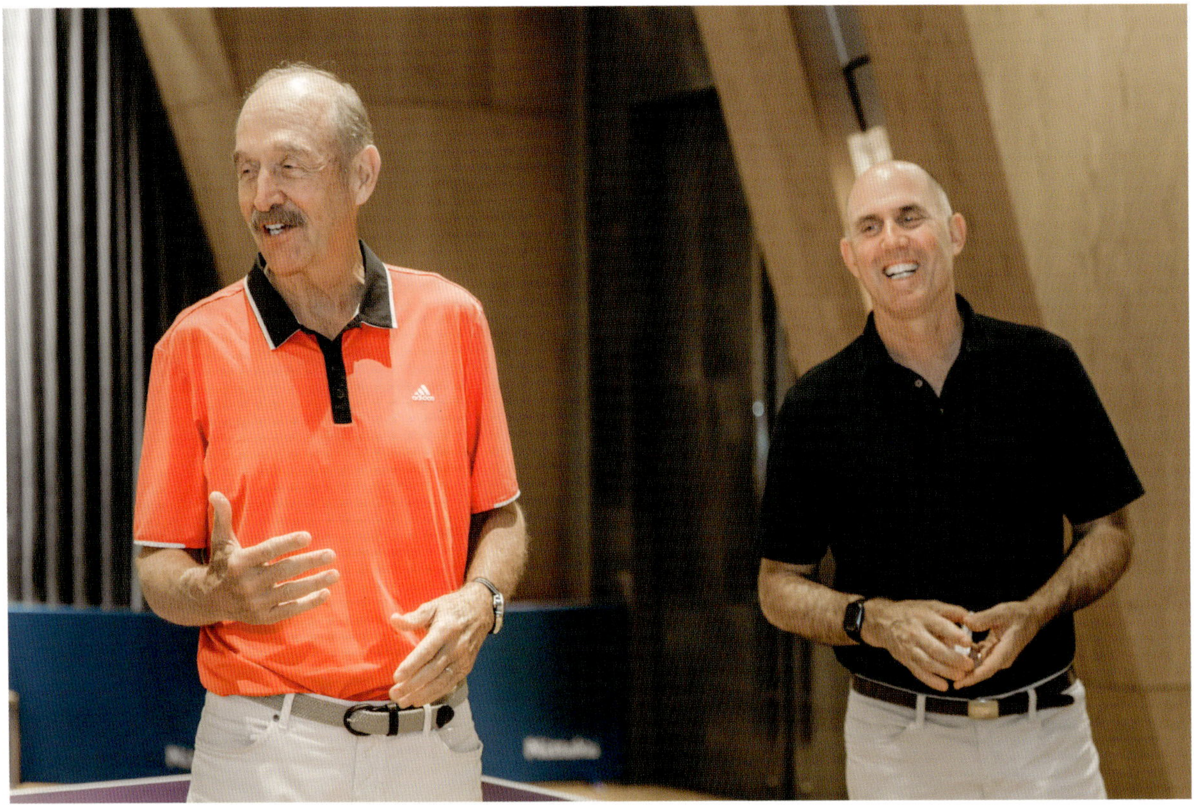

WINNING TRUST
HOW TO CREATE MOMENTS THAT MATTER

---

06 FOREWORD: A NOTE FROM DANNY MEYER

11 THE FIRST SERVE

43 **STRATEGIZE:** DESIGN MOMENTS THAT MATTER

69 **ENGAGE:** OPEN HEARTS

99 **RECREATE:** PLAY TOGETHER

129 **VOLLEY:** RALLY YOUR WAY FORWARD

159 **ELEVATE:** CHASE DOWN EVERY BALL

189 SECOND SERVES

199 TRY YOUR SERVE

213 ACKNOWLEDGEMENTS

FOREWORD

A NOTE FROM DANNY MEYER

Years before I stepped into the world of restaurants, I was standing towards the front of a tour bus, bumping along the streets of Rome with a microphone in my hand. My dad had a group tour business there; at the age of 20, I was one of his guides.

As my guests hobbled off their overnight flights, jet-lagged and catching their bearings, I doled out chilled aperitifs and conversation. I would spot the crankiest ones and figure out how I could win them over. I'd find the happiest ones and dream up ways to make them even happier. I knew Italy fairly well at that point, my nose to the ground as I searched out the best trattorias, caffès with perfect espresso, restaurants run by the most hospitable families. I tried to give my guests all the unique experiences I had discovered myself: adding in a few stops that weren't on their printed itineraries, arranging a memorable meal well off the beaten path. I knew I had both the opportunity and responsibility to make their experiences ones they would never forget. So at twenty years old, it was hospitality boot camp. It became one of those pivotal experiences in my life that taught me how to take care of people—even the ones you have to work hard to win over.

Both then and since, I've also learned about the power of hospitality with intention. A meaningful experience hinges on careful groundwork, the layering of details, and thoughtfully creating something that will hopefully end with people saying, "At that moment in time, there's nowhere in the world I would have rather been." There's no team I would rather work alongside. There's no business I'd rather trust.

When I met Stan Smith and Gary Niebur, I knew it going to be a joyous ride. Immediately I noted their optimism, their authentic concern for others, and their ability to not only design and execute incredible events but to connect people to one another in the process. It's like they hold a magic wand above their guests wherever they go, and everyone ends up with pixie dust on their shoulders. Stan and Gary know how to hold people together; they fill space with warmth and camaraderie. And they are as far as you can get from "just add water." Theirs is a world of nuance, of beauty, and of seasoned intentionality.

FOREWORD

FOREWORD

FOREWORD

As you might expect, they also have an athletic spirit—they lunge forward with bright eyes and unwavering belief. They've been raised on finely tuned strategy, self-discipline, and high expectations. I don't know how many tennis matches they've won in their respective careers, how many trophies line their cases, or how many times they've created events that resulted in dramatic relational and financial success for their clients. But I know that time and time again they've won with me.

I once believed I was primarily in the business of serving good food. What I discovered, though, is that food is secondary to something that matters even more: how we make people *feel*. If we make it our business to create positive, uplifting outcomes for human experiences and human relationships, we'll hit those transformative notes. Our work, no matter what shape it takes, will matter. Stan and Gary get this. And they've spent their adult lives (and this book) opening that same door to you.

Winning Trust isn't for a select few. They're inviting all of us onto the court and showing us how to SERVE, and how to create moments that people will walk away from saying, "There's nowhere I would have rather been."

I can say it with all confidence: these are the kind of men you want by your side.

—DANNY MEYER

"Life is moment, after moment, after moment. Let's create ones that matter."

—STAN SMITH & GARY NIEBUR

THE FIRST SERVE

WE ALL WANT A LIFE THAT MATTERS. We long for significance—and we're hoping and believing that whatever we're leaning our weight into will have lasting impact. Once we have some solid years of living under our belt, we usually end up recognizing that our significance is less tied to the "what" and more tied to the "who." When we invest in other humans, building trust and substance in those relationships, we have foundations that weather life's inevitable storms. We build partnerships and connections that are honoring and substantial with generational impact. We create teams who run confidently toward a vision because we have each other's backs, regardless of daily wins or losses. We form families who want to stick together and marriages that hold steady. We leave legacies that don't just exist on paper; they're written on hearts.

Recently we were gathered at a table in London. We had just watched some incredible tennis on the grassy courts of Wimbledon. Andre Agassi had openly shared his life's journey with our small group of clients and their guests, setting the stage for the evening. Afterwards, conversation at the tables was floating between individuals: some who knew each other well, some more newly acquainted, and all who had brought spouses or partners to share in the weekend experience. Our client saw the chance, in that moment, to build off the momentum Agassi had created with his storytelling. Our client encouraged others to share their own stories—and at each table, eyes lit up. The stories that followed were tender, funny, prized. The door was open for high engagement because we had been intentional about creating space for connection. When we parted ways that evening, it was clear we had shared a moment that mattered.

This moment around the table wouldn't have happened without everything that occurred leading up to it. Creating that moment took thoughtful strategy, a desirable invitation, focused elements to delight guests, a unique environment and warm atmosphere, and elevating the experience with finely-executed details to show every guest their value.

And that's what this book is all about:

creating moments that matter with the people who matter, because it's in this space where connections deepen and trust is won.

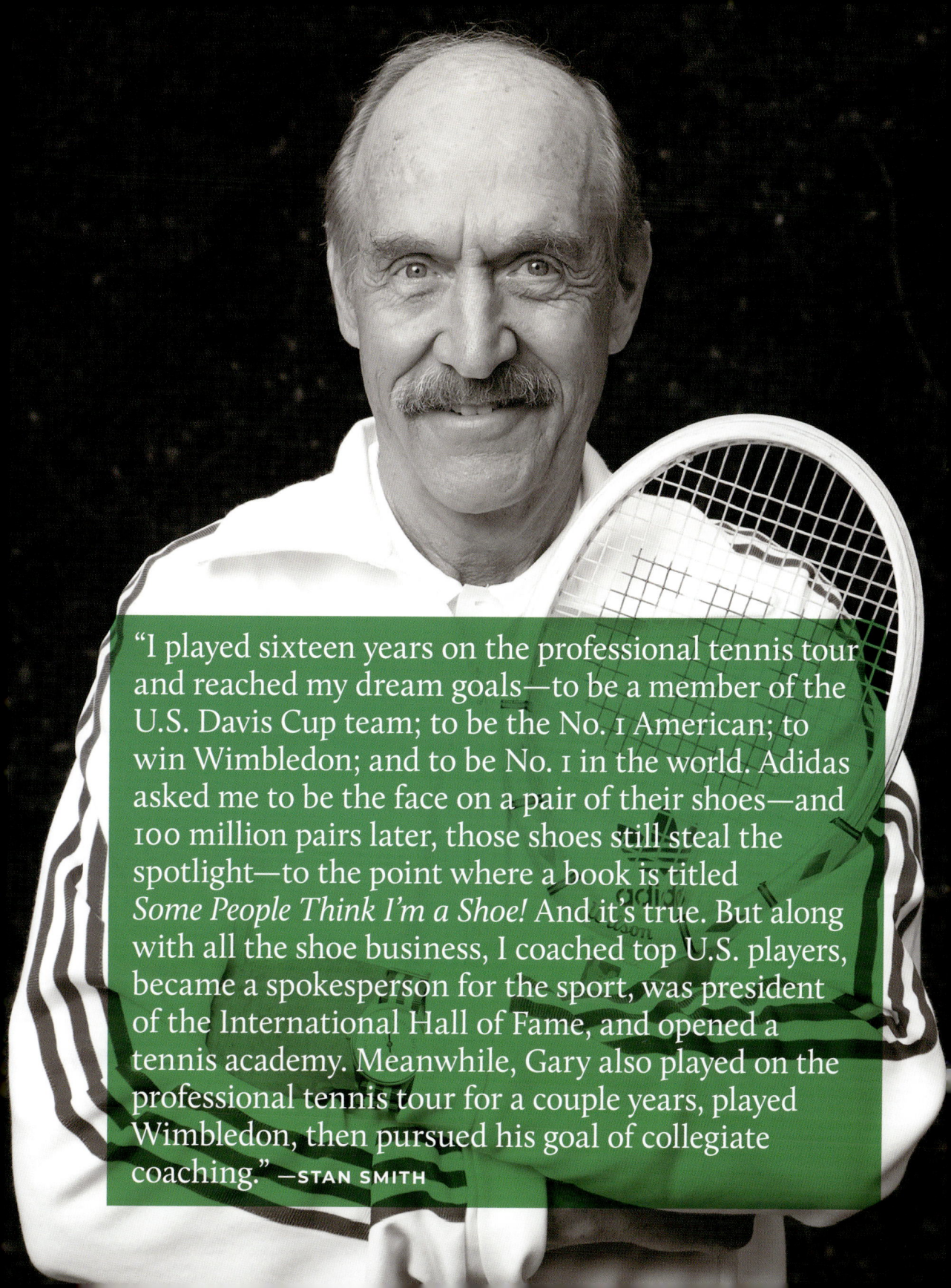

"I played sixteen years on the professional tennis tour and reached my dream goals—to be a member of the U.S. Davis Cup team; to be the No. 1 American; to win Wimbledon; and to be No. 1 in the world. Adidas asked me to be the face on a pair of their shoes—and 100 million pairs later, those shoes still steal the spotlight—to the point where a book is titled *Some People Think I'm a Shoe!* And it's true. But along with all the shoe business, I coached top U.S. players, became a spokesperson for the sport, was president of the International Hall of Fame, and opened a tennis academy. Meanwhile, Gary also played on the professional tennis tour for a couple years, played Wimbledon, then pursued his goal of collegiate coaching." —STAN SMITH

Before we dove into this world of creating and hosting moments that matter, we were eating, sleeping, and breathing the world of professional tennis. We poured our lives into the pursuit of big dreams both on and off the court.

Then our lives began to overlap.

> "After coaching, I started a company that included exclusive-access trips to Wimbledon for special guests and friends. One of those friends asked if I could do the same thing for his business—his key clients. I agreed, and I felt it made sense to invite someone who had won Wimbledon to host this event with me. That person was Stan. The event was a huge success. One of the attendees, a COO of a major airline, said, 'I've been coming to Wimbledon for thirty years, but never like this.' It was an *aha* moment. While Stan and I were sitting in the players' lounge, an idea sparked: we could take what we'd just done at Wimbledon and apply it to the Olympics. We could give people unique access to athletes who would engage with them—gold medalists who would share their stories, join them in the stands, teach them about what judges are looking for and the fine details of an athlete's performance.

We believed this kind of atmosphere, this way of giving people access to people and places they couldn't get on their own, would be significant in deepening relationships between clients and their guests.

And if we engaged people well in the midst of a premier experience, it would mirror what had just happened at Wimbledon. It would stand out in the sea of corporate events." —Gary Niebur

adidas
PALACE
SMITH
STEARNS
TENNIS ACADEMY
adidas

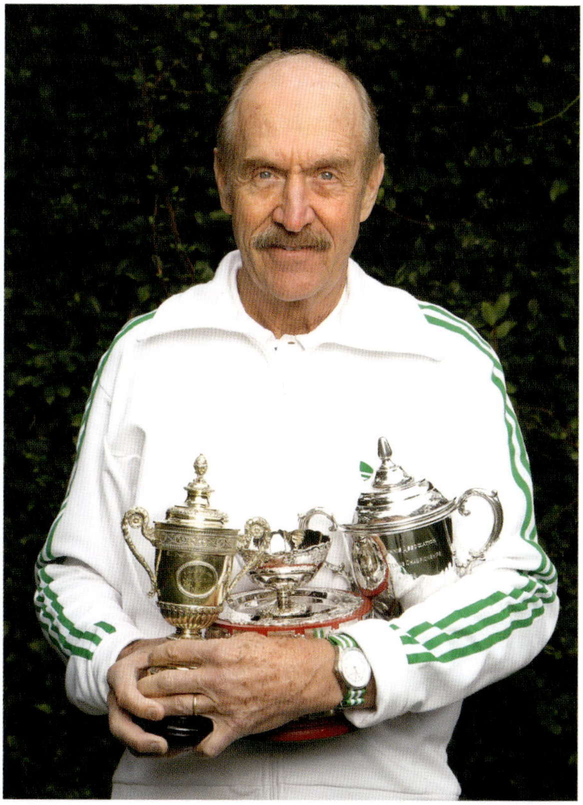

Gary
Gary Niebur
PRE-WIMBLEDON BREAKFAST
Magda

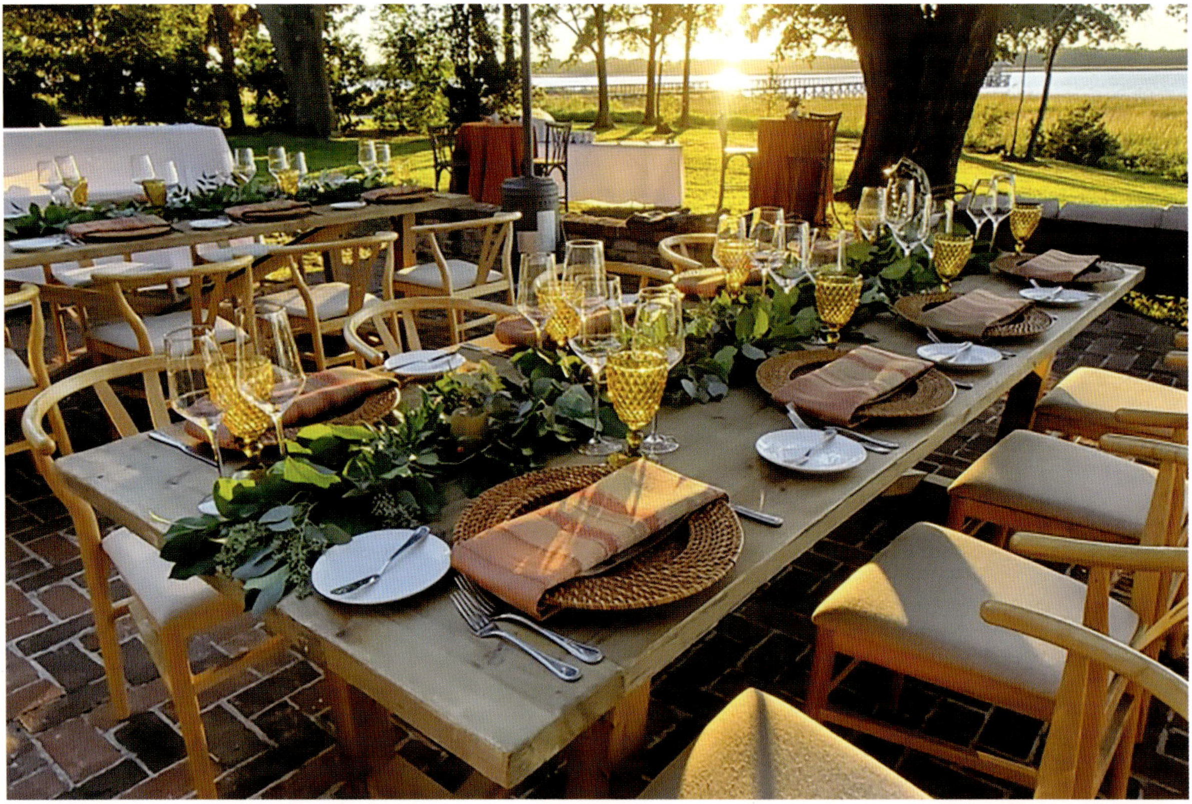

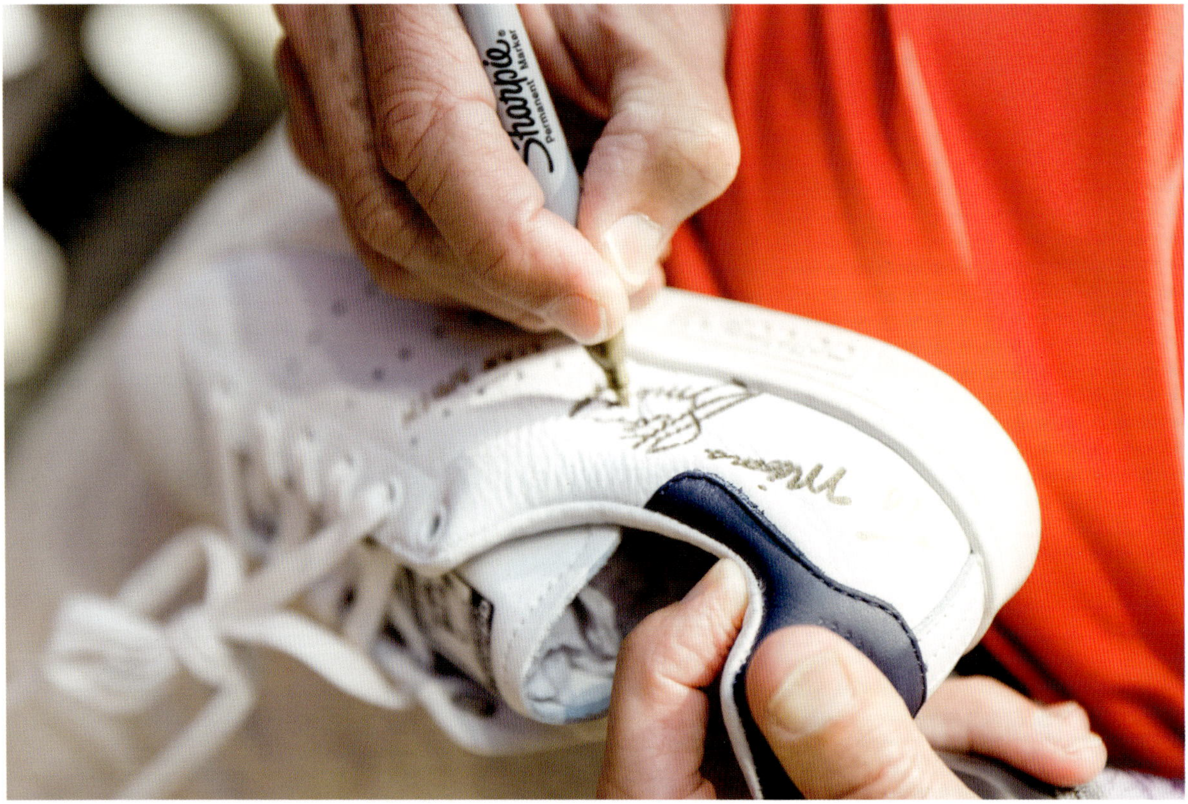
Sharpie
Permanent Marker

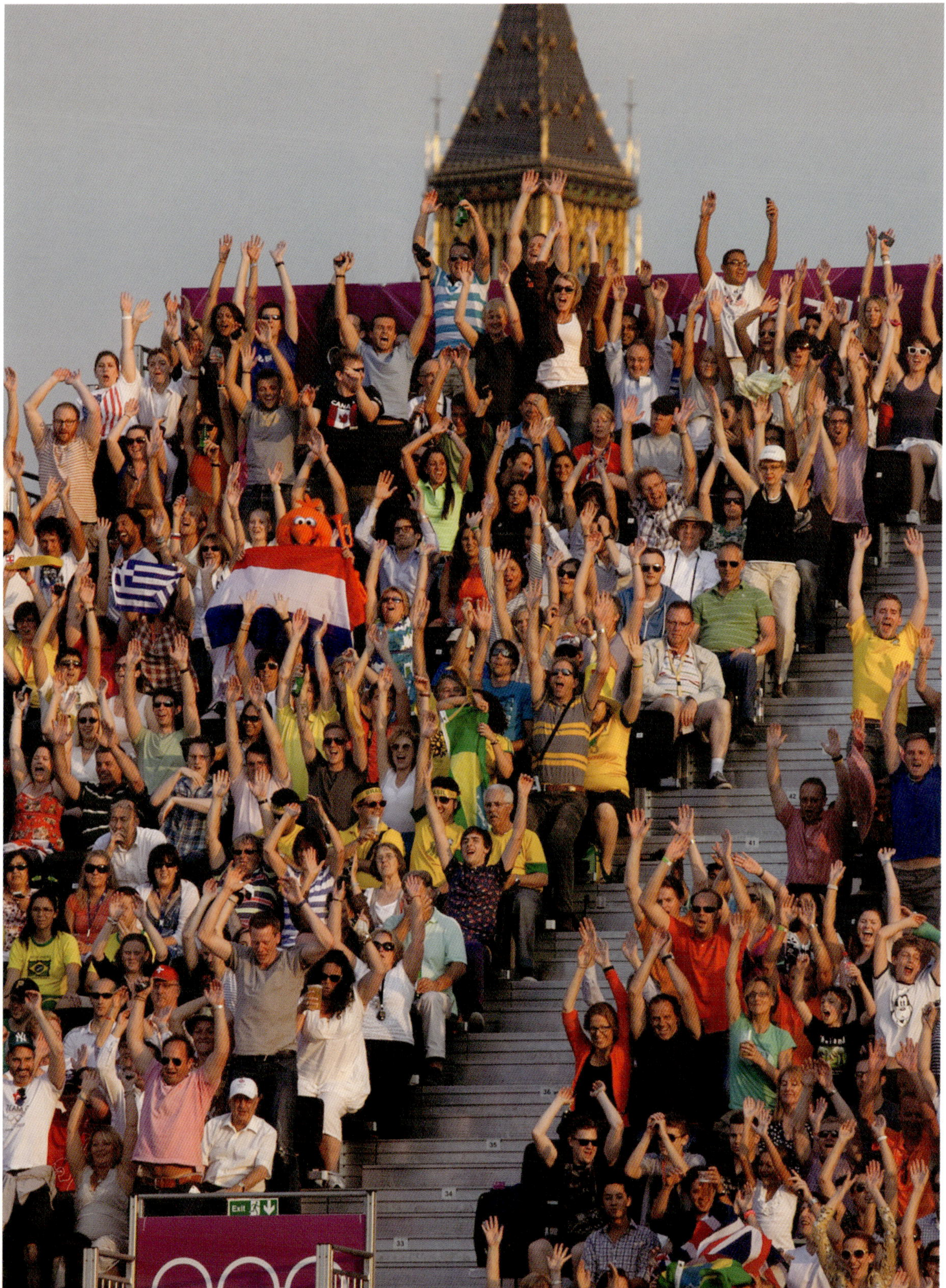
Exit

And that's when someone introduced us to Kay Wight.

Kay Wight was with American Express at the time, and she was in search of a partner to create a vision for their hospitality program at the 1996 Olympics in Atlanta. Even though Kay had most of the event and logistics details in place, she believed the program could still be enhanced. She wanted to go outside the box, create something that was highly relational, boutique, and would create an environment that would help American Express leadership engage with their partners. We told her about what we'd just created around Wimbledon in 1995, and she was thrilled. She asked us to be the ones to elevate their existing plan and turn it into a big moment that mattered.

We put all our ideas on the table and brainstormed how to surprise and delight our new client and their invitees in a way that felt unique and set apart from the standard event. We found beautiful homes around Atlanta where we could host intimate dinners, with Olympic gold medalists joining us around the dinner table. We turned a spacious garage into a gymnastics exhibition, and Nadia Comaneci and Bart Conner did routines right in front of our delighted guests. We elevated every detail we could think of, hiring coaches and personal trainers to teach tennis and golf to our guests, giving them the chance to participate and not just be bystanders. We designed fun team challenges, handed out customized awards and gifts, and capped off the experience by standing alongside our client and sharing with guests why we did what we did, how we value one another, and the bonds we formed. For the closing dinner, our gold medal athletes returned to share a last dinner with us, surprising guests and turning it into a memorable finale.

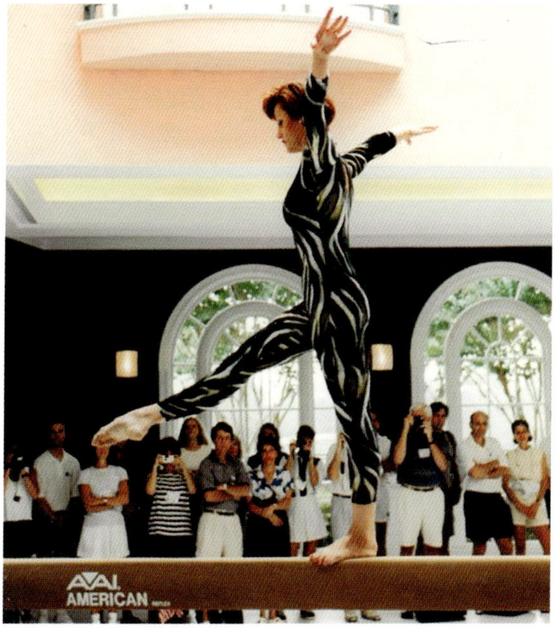
AMERICAN

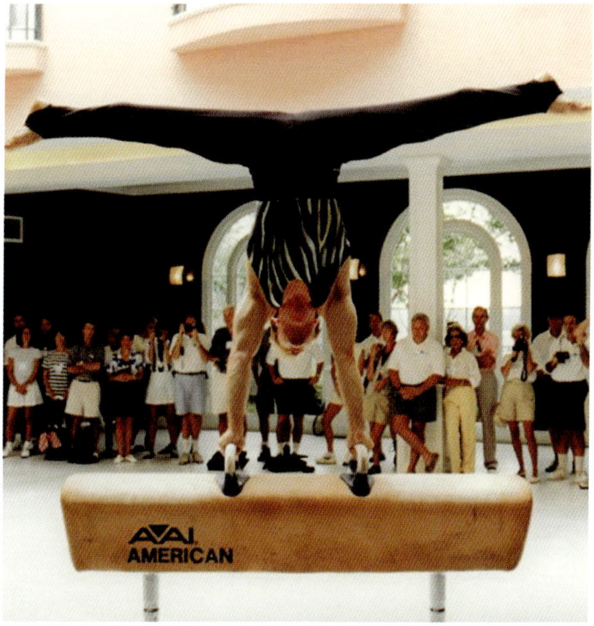
AMERICAN

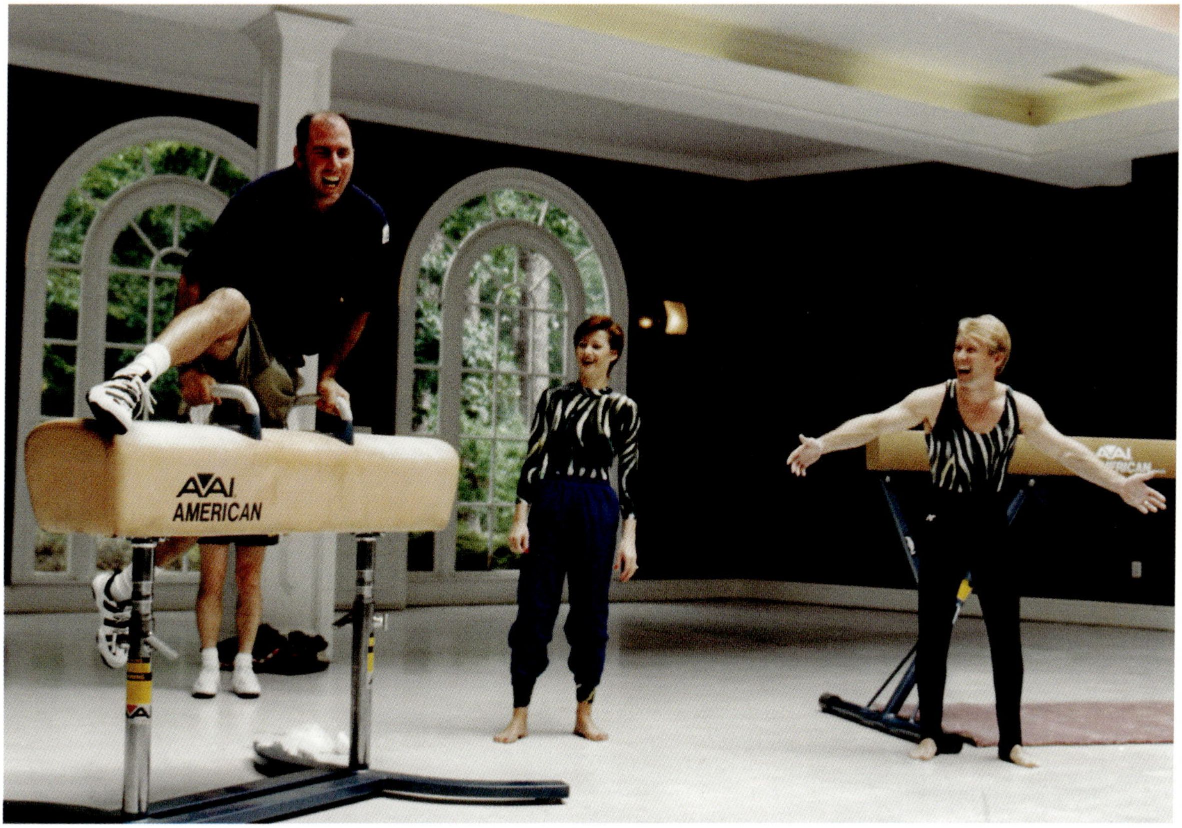
AMERICAN

"I've done a million corporate outings, but these are different. It's never transactional or superficial. Being part of this team is like immediately coming into a family."

—DAVIS LOVE III, 1997 PGA CHAMPION, 1992 AND 2003 PLAYERS CHAMPIONSHIPS, 2012 AND 2016 RYDER CUP CAPTAIN, 2022 PRESIDENTS CUP CAPTAIN AND 2017 WORLD GOLF HALL OF FAME

We were able to help a client earn deeper trust with their valued guests. We went outside the box of a typical corporate event. Most importantly, we helped Kay create a series of moments that mattered, accelerating trust in her company's most important business relationships.

Seeing that impact unfold, it felt like we were onto something.

We had a wonderful, experienced partner join us early on, Don Baer, who affirmed that if we were going to build a lasting position in the premier event space, we would need to discover a model where everything could feel special, even if we were running the same sort of program year after year. He cautioned us about growing too fast or too big and encouraged us to set boundaries so that our marriages and family relationships would stay our top priority. Ultimately, we had to model what it looked like to value relationships and steward the moments that matter in life, and for us that started at home.

From the start, we've limited how many events we do each year so overgrowth won't happen, and so every experience we create has our team's full attention and can land in the boutique category. We're driven to be so excellent and customized with what we design that repeat business is the norm. We focus on making sure everyone who comes into contact with our team and one of our events—whether client, guest, talent, or partner—is given a uniquely personal experience that ends in a stronger relationship between us and our clients.

THE FIRST SERVE

"Don't miss the opportunity to create those next-level connections between people, whether it happens around a table, on a pickleball court, or in the stands. Make relationships your strategy. It's the best investment you'll make." —GARY NIEBUR

Gary Niebur

We're both cut from the same competitive cloth, so once we hung the Stan Smith Events sign outside our door, we wanted to operate our business at the same level we approached the game of tennis itself. We asked probing questions of corporate leaders and their teams to understand what was working and not working in the realm of corporate events. We wanted to see what significantly moved the needle forward between clients and their guests. We got sound advice and keen help from our spouses, who came alongside us in so many ways with their own expertise. We prayed for wisdom, sought out mentors, asked more questions.

We believed that if we could help people—in our case, corporate leaders—design elevated (even personalized) experiences to invite others into, those experiences would have significant impact on their most valuable relationships. The experience would deepen bonds and establish trust at a more rapid pace, both inside and outside their business. And we heard again and again that business leaders need and want these tethered connections, but also need someone to help them get there.

As Kevin Warren, one of our clients and trusted friends, shared with us:

> "When you're early in your career, working as an individual or with a small team, you can likely muscle your way through. But as you go up and go wide, now you're working with partners and clients. And it is ALL about people—investing in their lives, picking and developing them as part of your team, being there for them in real ways. When you invest in people, they will take the hill with you."
> —**KEVIN WARREN, FORMER FORTUNE 100 CMO**

THE FIRST SERVE

We need people to take the hill with us—not because it's listed in their job description or by some obligatory contract, but because they have a genuine desire to do so. We need teams, partners, and individuals who will rally alongside us because they're connected to us in a meaningful and personal way. Getting to that depth of relational connection is, therefore, critical.

Whether you're CEO of a Fortune 500 or a start-up, whether you lead a global team or a neighborhood nonprofit, whether you manage a household or a hotel, it can be a lot to shoulder. You know the burdens and intense level of responsibility in the day-to-day operations and routine. Maybe it's difficult to imagine having the space and time to invest more to create moments that matter. But we believe it's those intentionally designed and executed moments that will get us where we long to be: to have trusted, authentic connections in our most valued relationships. And these connections will lead to more fulfilling days— and a more dynamic, meaningful life.

We began to believe that we could be the partner that could help clients seize moments that matter, accelerate relationship formation, and ultimately win trust.

Now, after a few decades of creating events and experiences in high-stakes relationships, we've distilled our process into five core elements: our SERVE framework. Obviously rich in meaning, SERVE captures both the nature of building lasting relationships—leading with an others-first mentality—and also the most important shot in a tennis match. To win, you must SERVE well. We believe this framework enables you to do both; and if you develop the practice of SERVE, you will find that every relationship in your life (not just in business) has the opportunity to go deeper, to accelerate the formation of lasting connection, and over time, to win trust.

WELCOME TO SERVE.

STRATEGIZE: DESIGN MOMENTS THAT MATTER
Use your team and resources to plan a unique, delightful atmosphere that opens up the opportunity to win trust in important relationships.

ENGAGE: OPEN HEARTS
Care about and engage with the whole person—not just the transaction or business deal—so each client and guest feels known, valued, and comfortable in any given situation.

RECREATE: PLAY TOGETHER
Build bonds and shared memories through fun experiences like team challenges and mini tournaments. Guards come down; trust grows.

VOLLEY: RALLY YOUR WAY FORWARD
Problem-solve with direction and optimism—letting ideas flow without defensiveness or ego—so the end result both solidifies trust and innovates into new spaces.

ELEVATE: CHASE DOWN EVERY BALL
Nail every detail so the entire experience exceeds expectations with special invitations, unique access, customized gifts, or surprise moments that solidify a trusted relationship.

Within this book, we'll unpack these five core elements of SERVE and give you three simple action steps within each one to help you move forward. We operate and have operated within a very specific domain—with specific kinds of clients, access, and experiences that are way outside the norm of day-to-day business and life. However, we believe the principles behind what we do can apply to any relationship and any context. We'll share these moments with you, but **you will have your own venues, your own resources, your own gifts, your own unique spin on where to take this.** You will be able to take our principles and the stories surrounding them and apply them to your own life in ways we haven't yet imagined.

Some of this SERVE framework comes from what we learned from parents, mentors, and spiritual leaders—from what they taught us about seeing all people the way God sees them, with immense and equal value. Some of the framework has been discovered with our families as we've learned how to strengthen bonds with one another by getting outside of our routines to play games, recreate, and invest in memorable experiences. Some of the framework has come through observing, working with, and learning from our clients and event partners as we see how they identify and steward moments that matter. And some of what you'll see in our framework comes from what we gleaned as tennis players and coaches—how to design strategy, chase down and sweat the details, push through mistakes, and take a second serve.

Maybe creating significant experiences feels easy for you, and you've already put a few of these practices in place with whoever you're leading or working alongside. This book may help you get over the next hurdle or shed light on a method you hadn't yet envisioned. Maybe you never quite had a foundation of trust, and you're about to hit a milestone moment and need to build it intentionally and with earnestness. Maybe you're approaching a critical moment in your business or life and you know that trust is absent—you can sense the uneasiness or rocky ground—but you don't know how to create anything better than what you've got. Maybe you've lost trust in a relationship and need to bring it back. **So often we can identify the moment that matters but don't know how to make something come of it.** We believe you can get there, and that this framework will help.

THE FIRST SERVE

To reveal how SERVE works in the real world, we're going to share stories: our own, ones from clients, ones from our team, ones from partners. We hope these stories will help show you the nuance of how trust is deepened, how it transforms us in surprising ways, how it heals old habits and prevents future breakdowns. We also want to honor the people who have welcomed us into their lives and businesses, trusting us to do good work alongside them. We hope that sharing these stories will help guide your own.

So here's one to start us off—a story that shows the fullness of a SERVE:

> "I was dodging traffic on Madison Avenue, hurrying to get to my seat at the US Open, when Stuart called. I could tell by his tone that it was critical.
>
> Stan and I met Stuart years earlier—we were swinging rackets on the grass courts across from Wimbledon, connecting Stuart and our other guests to some of the best tennis stars in the world—and we began bouncing ideas around about how to accelerate trust in the corporate space. Then 2020 rolled around.
>
> Stuart's company, Computershare, had just acquired a sizable division from a massive bank. Computershare helps companies with the administration and management of equities, and they'd been looking for an opportunity to expand into the US markets. Negotiating the deal was challenging enough, but the real work was about to begin.
>
> In the wake of an acquisition, investors often experience a wave of anxiety like jumping out of an airplane, waiting for the chute to open. There's a rush of adrenaline from the promise of upside—that's what leads them to pursue the deal in the first place. But there's also a risk of downside—that's what motivated the seller to get out. Stuart was hovering in that space where the upside either unfolds and carries you to a safe, prosperous landing or something malfunctions and it all crashes into the ground.

To make matters even more difficult, the world was locked down by a global pandemic. And trust-building rituals like dinners and handshakes were replaced by awkward, technology-challenged video calls between home-bound employees. To make the acquisition work, Stuart needed to earn the buy-in of an executive team whose own circumstances seemed designed to convince them that they should trust no one.

They'd spent years as a peripheral arm inside a financial institution with many balls of its own to juggle: industry regulations, intense competition, and a rapidly evolving customer base. The effort to sustain the core banking business was so demanding, it often left this division feeling like neglected misfits fighting for relevance… orphans in their own family. And now this team of executives was receiving the news that they'd been sold to an Australian group about whom they knew very little. Would they fit the new culture? Would their jobs be continued? And even if they were, would they end up wishing they weren't? What were their plans for this organization?

> To make the acquisition work, Stuart needed to earn the buy-in of an executive team whose own circumstances seemed designed to convince them that they should trust no one.

Stuart needed to build a trust strong enough to bear the mounting load of doubt and suspicion surrounding it. That kind of trust usually comes from a decades-long track record of character and reliability. But Stuart didn't have decades to create it. His company already had an excellent culture, but the new team needed to experience it to believe it.

So there in the heart of New York City traffic, Stuart and I started volleying ideas back and forth on how to quickly win trust from the management team he'd just acquired after a merger that happened over Zoom. The ten newly acquired key executives were on edge. So Stuart had two teams who had never met, had no understanding of each other, no connection, and no foundation of trust. Stuart knew he had only a sliver of time to either keep or lose them. And he desperately wanted them to stay.

One idea led to the next. Stuart knew he needed the right environment to reveal his company's culture, and I bounced back ideas on what Stan Smith Events could bring to the table: what type of venue might thrill people, what talent to bring in, what genuine moments of connection we could build by recreating. Stuart and I had begun playing tennis—without the racket—by staying humble and open to each other's perspectives. We ended the call, and our team quickly jumped in, designing a detailed and executable plan on an accelerated timeline. We landed on where we'd gather, eat, relax, recreate, connect.

When the weekend came for Stuart's two teams to meet, and we had all the details locked into place, the momentum began. Stan engaged everyone immediately, making everyone feel welcomed and included. Stuart never brought up work, just engaged with each person and set the tone for true camaraderie. We all got together on a tennis court—even the ones who had never lifted a racket—and Stan and I gave lessons to every skill level, laughing and self-deprecating, then ending with a playful awards ceremony. We hiked, golfed, shared amazing meals and conversation. We surprised the guests with gifts left in their room while they were at dinner; we gave everyone a pair of autographed Stan Smith shoes in their size. The trust bridge was being built. Stuart's genuine care for his new team was like a beacon.

"...what type of venue might thrill people, what talent to bring in, what genuine moments of connection we could build by recreating."

Weeks later, their merged team of twenty was moving forward as an engaged, empowered unit, laser-focused on a set of objectives that would eventually produce significant revenue and an impressive ROI for the company. Those results were clear. But what we also knew was that underneath the newly-built trust was a group of people who had the potential to carry that trust forward to their own reports, their own key moments, their own relationships."

—Gary Niebur

> "...underneath the newly-built trust was a group of people who had the potential to carry that trust forward to their own reports."

As you flip through these stories like Stuart's, you may be drawn to one SERVE principle or another. You may find you already do some of these elements exceptionally well, but have never considered others. You might be pro level at engaging hearts but haven't built a team that can elevate the details. You may have been born with a knack for giving memorable gifts but haven't considered how pushing your chair back from your desk and picking up a ping-pong paddle could be your key to next-level partnership or team unity.

This book is our way of inviting anyone who's interested in creating moments that matter into the workrooms of Stan Smith Events, into the conversations we've had with incredible leaders and talent, and into the front seat of our Sprinter vans as we journey from points A to Z.

Not a day passes that we don't believe in the work our team is getting to do. We get to host events for incredible clients while working with renowned athletes, restaurateurs, sommeliers, CEOs, and international talent. We have the honor of partnering with phenomenal venue staff, reliable drivers, hospitality gurus and caterers, and our own wonderful family members who bridge every gap. We've also had the immense fortune to have teammates and partners who linked arms with us early on to help us grow what we have to this day.

> "We didn't know this company was going to do what it did or have the effect it has had. We are so grateful. And we've learned through our faith that it's important to be wise stewards of what we've been given. We want to give away what we've learned to the next generation."
> —**GARY NIEBUR**

THE FIRST SERVE

Imagine we're handing you a racket right now. A fresh can of tennis balls. Plus a pair of Stan Smith Adidas shoes in your size. **We're excited and ready to coach you into identifying, capturing, and making the most of the moments that matter in your own relationships.** Let's start with a SERVE.

It's an honor to be on the court with you.

WHOSE TRUST DO YOU NEED TO WIN THIS YEAR? (MAKE A LIST SOMEWHERE, EVEN IF IN THE BACK OF THIS BOOK, AND HOLD ONTO IT.)

WHOSE TRUST DO YOU ALREADY HAVE? (WELL DONE.)

THE FIRST SERVE

"Partnering with your Stan Smith Events team—it's so elevated. Your attention to detail and planning well in advance is one of the biggest differentiators between how you approach events and what you normally get in this corporate event space. I don't just hand you a brief, ask you to plan it, then hope for the best. The whole nature of how we work together, sometimes a year in advance, is very interactive, very partnering. Which I love because I do not like surprises. Even positive surprises. As a host of an event, I want to stay in sync with the planning throughout, and you honor that. You also picked an amazing team who truly cares and shares your values. They're willing to push back with thoughtful challenge because of what they've learned along the way. I can get a little overboard with the business content, but early on when we started partnering, you guys were like, 'Yes, that content is spectacular, but let's make sure your guests are also going to have fun and experience something really memorable.' You all do a phenomenal job at this."

—ED OLEBE, FORTUNE 100 PRESIDENT

"When I first heard of you guys, it was because my boss, Gordon Smith, said I had to call you. I was in a CFO position, so I was in that cost-control mindset. I was skeptical and thought we had people on our team who knew how to run an event... so why go outside of that? But I called you, and immediately of course I liked you because you're so personable, and then we started planning an event around the US Open. We played with McEnroe, we did the luncheon out on the court with Danny Meyer.... It all turned out so great. I understood why we needed you. Your presence and ability to create special moments changed the event. It was the whole day that felt that way, from the arrival to the team challenge to the celebrities and interactions. You created all these avenues for people to be in their sweet spot. You design these events to break down those levels, those hierarchical things, and all of a sudden you're just people. I learned how much these kinds of relationships matter early in my career, but it was just tucked away. Then it was rekindled by Gordon Smith, who was just incredible at engaging and caring for people, and it became a defining part of how I work, and how I approach my career."

—MICHAEL RITTLER, FORMER FORTUNE 100 AND 500 GM

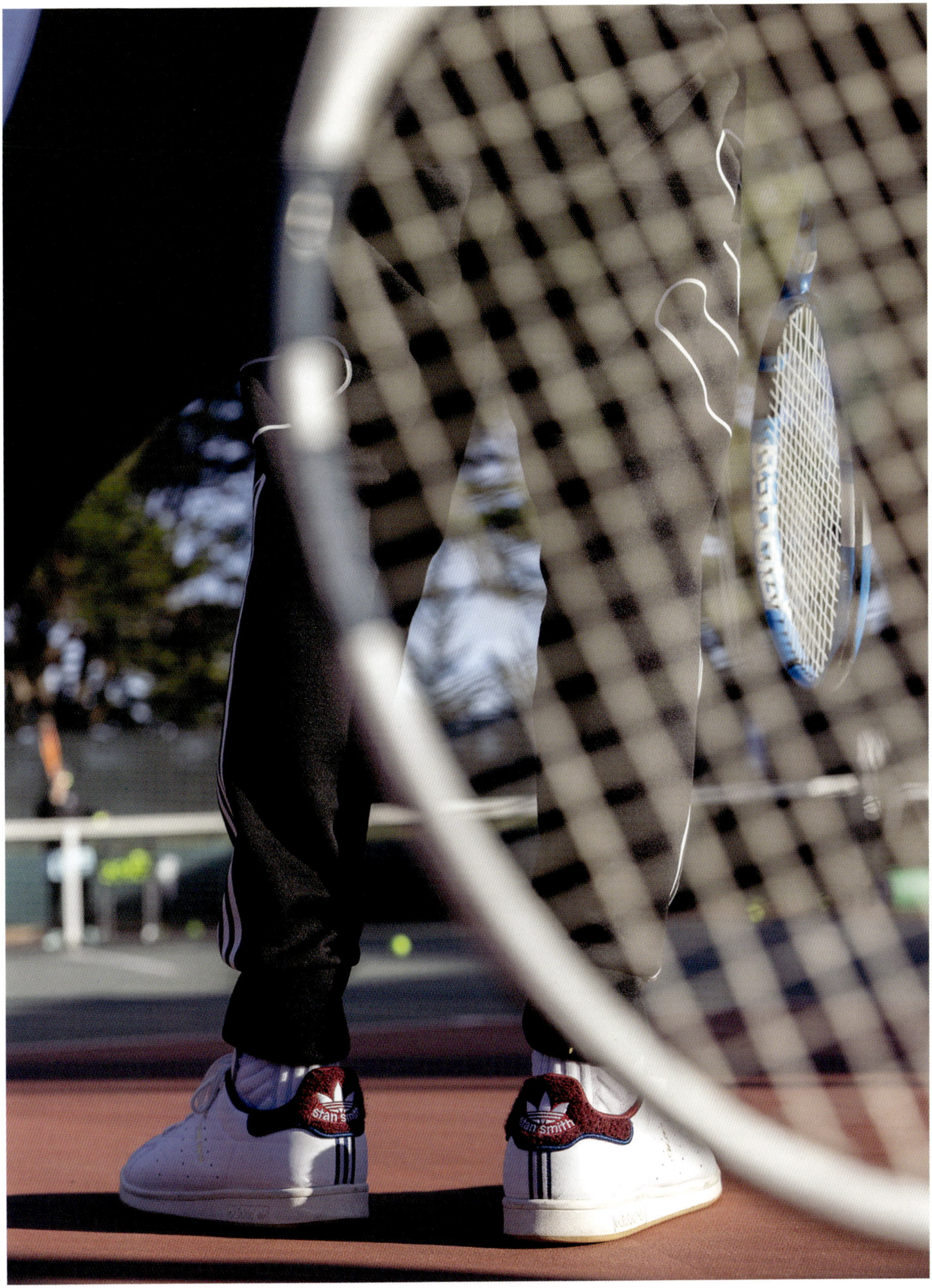
stan smith
stan smith

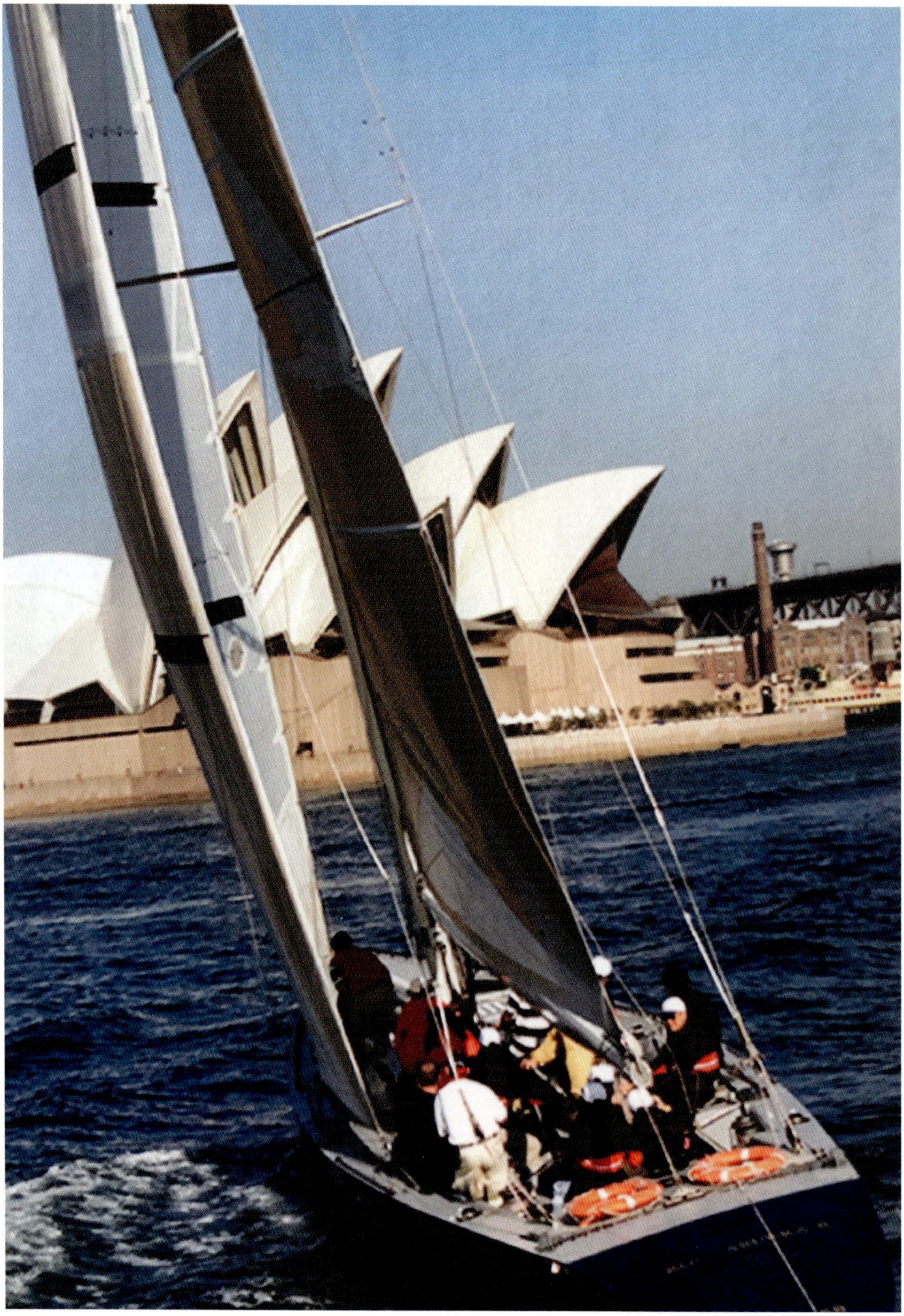

"The word 'partner' is sometimes overused, but that's what this is—a genuine partnership. I trust you as individuals; I trust your business. It's very special when you have something like this."

—KEVIN WARREN

"I never walked onto a tennis court without a strategy." —STAN SMITH

STRATEGIZE:
DESIGN MOMENTS THAT MATTER

Use your team and resources to plan a unique, delightful atmosphere that opens up the opportunity to win trust in important relationships.

WHEN DESIGNING MOMENTS THAT MATTER, the first step is to identify the opportunity—the relationship that's ripe for accelerating trust. Then it's time to carefully and creatively plan all the elements that will make the most of that opportunity.

Strategy is all the pre-event, pre-experience work. We join forces with our client and start by asking questions like:

Who's invited to this event—and how can we get them to say "yes"?
What time of year should this happen?
What unique location will delight people and has the right atmosphere?
What type of activities will loosen people up and break down walls, spark laughter and competition, generate connection?
What dining style is right for this specific group?
Who needs to sit by whom?
Should we invite couples or individuals?
What kind of surprise or gift will make someone feel seen and valued?
What's the budget?
What team resources can we put behind this?

STRATEGIZE

We dig in to get answers to all of these questions, without letting anything slip through the cracks if we can help it. If we don't know an answer, we will search and ask until we find it. As we get our arms around it, we slowly but surely narrow in on the key elements. These pieces of data and planning are so critical to lay the foundation for everything that follows within the event itself. In other words: "S" is what opens the door to a successful E (Engage), R (Recreate), V (Volley), and E (Elevate). Nail your strategy—your personalized plan for creating moments that matter. Then all the Engaging, Recreating, Volleying, and Elevating that follow will build momentum, create multiple pathways for connection, and swing wide the opportunities to accelerate trust right when and with whom you need it.

When strategizing: identify the pivotal moment, get to know your "who" (really well), and choose your hook.

"For the Stan Smith Events Team, our vendors and partners are so very important. Without their collaboration, we couldn't produce and execute the events we do. We trust each other. We've become friends." —MOLLY STEEVES, STAN SMITH EVENTS TEAM

STRATEGIZE

#1: IDENTIFY THE PIVOTAL MOMENT

In the first chapter, we shared Stuart's story and the critical need to build trust between teams. Stuart's story exemplifies how we identify the opportunity and then design moments that matter. Out of the gate, it was easy for us to see where trust needed to be established and accelerated in his scenario, as well as how significant the impact could be. The objective was clear; we could build the environment accordingly. We all identified that one immersive experience which, if executed well, would create a powerful and positive trajectory for both teams.

It's usually clear when a pivotal moment is on the horizon. You're merging teams, hiring a critical new employee, selling a company, speaking to a new audience, pursuing a big client or customer. On the flip side, maybe it's clear that you've lost trust and are sitting in that difficult valley. You know you've got a big climb ahead of you, so it's time to create an intentional experience as a way up and over the hill. These pivotal times are worth getting really strategic about, asking yourself how and when you'll accelerate trust—versus winging it or just assuming that eventually those relationships will fall into place. A passive stance won't bring the win. Every type of relationship requires care and effort if it's going to become a stabilizing force.

Stuart's was clearly a pivotal moment, but we're not all facing massive mergers. Sometimes moments seem smaller on the surface, but there's still something big on the line. It's the first day of school for your kids, you're promoting an employee, you're delivering difficult news—all of these are pivotal moments you can choose to either drift through or turn into something significant.

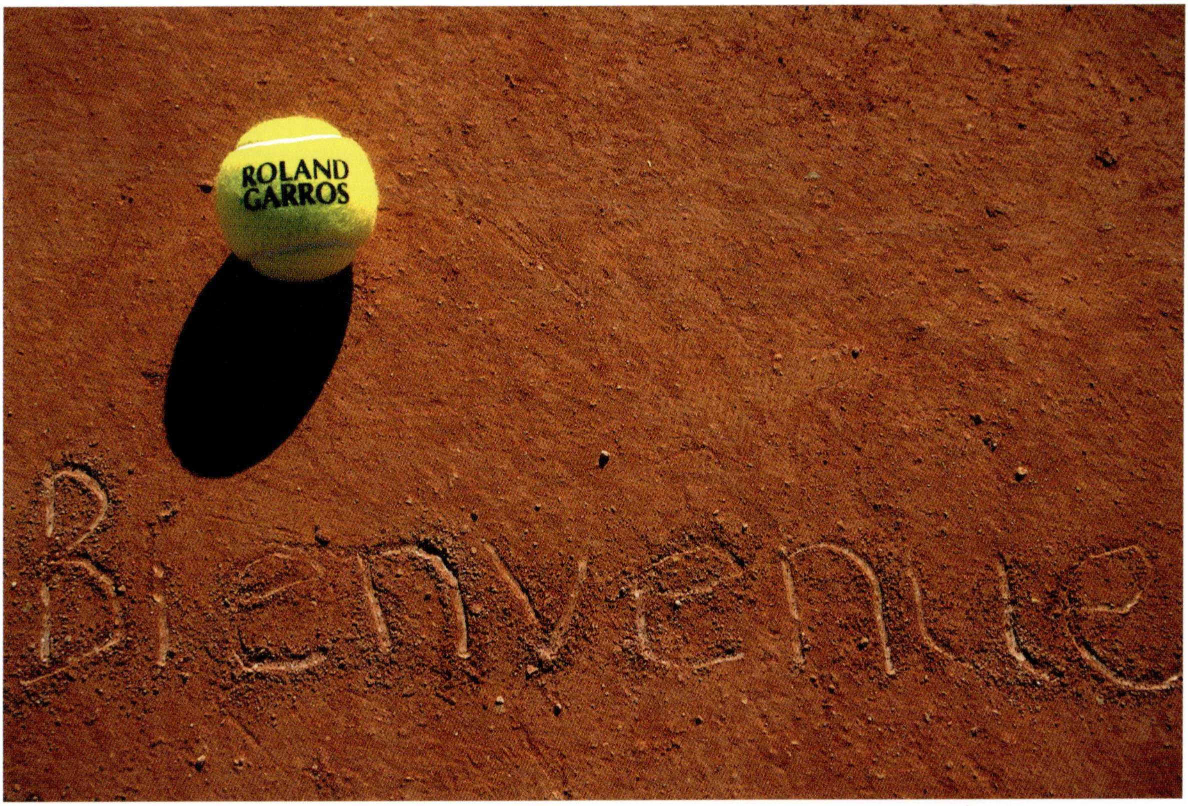
ROLAND
GARROS
Bienvenue

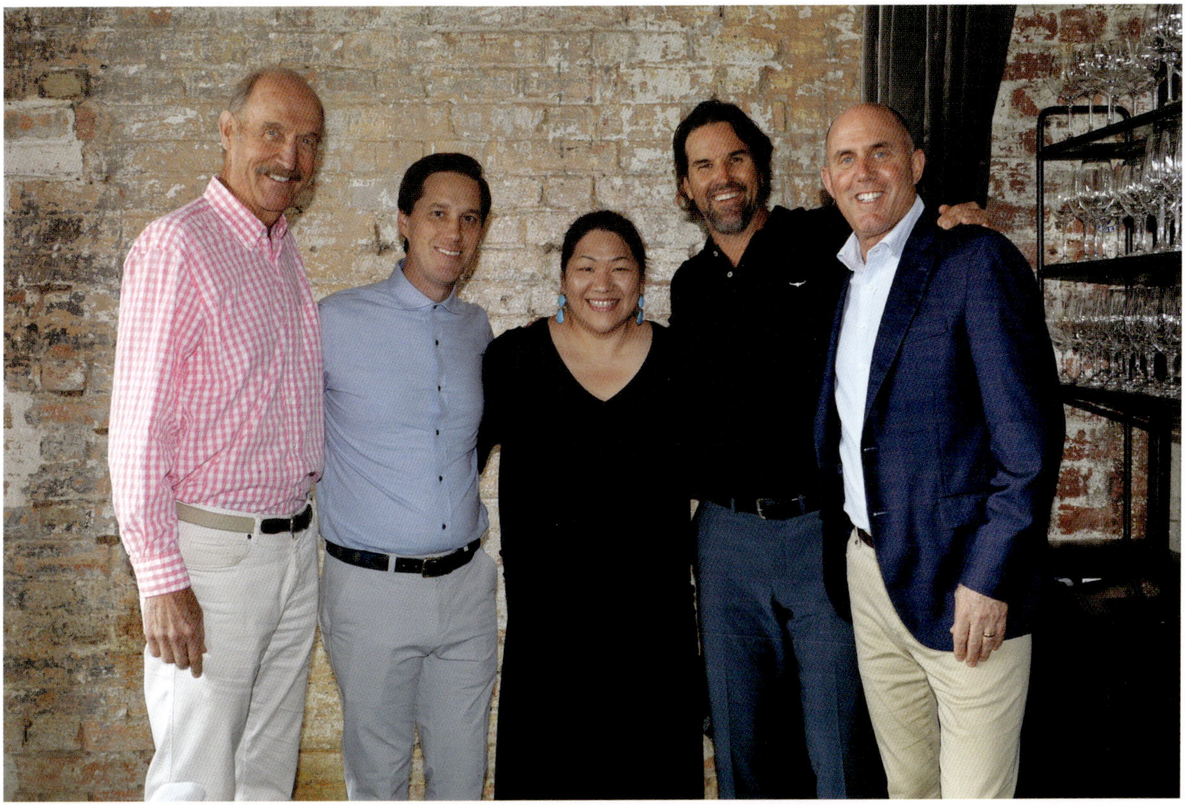

STRATEGIZE

"The strategic planning of the event was impeccable. Every day was as good if not better than the previous one. It was all so out of the ordinary and memorable… golf with Davis Love III, round robin tennis tournaments, games and prizes, dinner at the Love's house, and his daughter riding into the yard on horseback. Everything was so well planned and executed but never felt mechanical. It was authentic, transparent, heartwarming."

—RALPH ANDRETTA, PRESIDENT AND CEO FINANCIAL SERVICES

We often get asked by people who are trying to advance their careers, or who are new leaders, how to accelerate trust. We believe you can't even get to SERVE until you prove yourself reliable, a team player, a person worthy of being in charge. Even if you don't yet hold the title or resources, know that there are pivotal moments and opportunities where you can still model SERVE. Build and win trust on your team internally so you're trusted to do the same externally. Invite people to lunch and engage with them. Play a game together or join a league. Initiate good conversation and show genuine interest in others' lives outside of work. You'll be recognized for this if you show yourself faithful, and this step-by-step building of trust will have great future impact.

"WHOEVER CAN BE TRUSTED WITH VERY LITTLE CAN ALSO BE TRUSTED WITH MUCH." —JESUS (LUKE 16:10, HOLY BIBLE, NEW INTERNATIONAL VERSION)

"Don't undervalue uniqueness." —STAN SMITH

"You don't get access to the people you really need to influence without a well-strategized event. Not only do you get to entertain current customers or partners, but you get to entertain people who may have influence in the future. We partnered with Stan Smith Events at a Rugby World Cup in New Zealand, and we invited a guest who we knew was going to go on and do big things—and who we thought would really get excited about the weekend we planned. He came to the event, and four months later he was getting top awards. He was so sought-after that it would have been really difficult to get him at that point, but we had already established the relationship. These events create a level of loyalty that goes way beyond dollars and cents."

—TRACEY BOWRA, FORTUNE 100 GM

#2: KNOW YOUR WHO (REALLY WELL)

Once you've clearly identified your objective—why you're creating a moment that matters—you dig into the *who*.

We design the event with each guest in the forefront of our minds, and that gets the gears turning in a boutique way. All our guests are not delighted by the same locations, invitation, or access. It's our goal to figure out what has a high chance of making an experience really shine and exceed that person's expectations.

STRATEGIZE

WHO ARE THESE PEOPLE YOU'RE BRINGING AROUND THE SAME TABLE?

WHAT'S ON THAT WOMAN'S BUCKET LIST?

WHAT ACTIVITY WILL INSTILL A SENSE OF CAMARADERIE AMONGST INDIVIDUALS?

WHAT ATHLETE OR RESTAURANT WILL EXCEED EXPECTATIONS?

WOULD THIS PERSON OPEN UP TO HIS GUESTS FOR A FIRESIDE CHAT, OR DO WE NEED A HOST TO GUIDE CONVERSATION?

STRATEGIZE

WHEREVER YOU LIKE TO SAVE NOTES, FILL OUT THE FOLLOWING FOR A FAMILY MEMBER, FRIEND, OR CLIENT. (MAYBE YOU WON'T KNOW ALL THESE ANSWERS, BUT AIM FOR AT LEAST HALF.) THEN USING THE LIST, PLAN A MOMENT THAT MATTERS THAT INCLUDES A FEW OF THESE ELEMENTS.

HOBBIES

GAMES OR SPORTS THEY LOVE

NAMES OF FAMILY MEMBERS

FAVORITE BRANDS

GO-TO DRINK

PERSONAL HEROES

ALMA MATER

UPCOMING MILESTONES

FAVORITE PLACE TO EAT

SOMETHING THAT MAKES THEIR EYES LIGHT UP

SHOE SIZE

BIRTHDAY

BABY DUE DATE

ANNIVERSARY

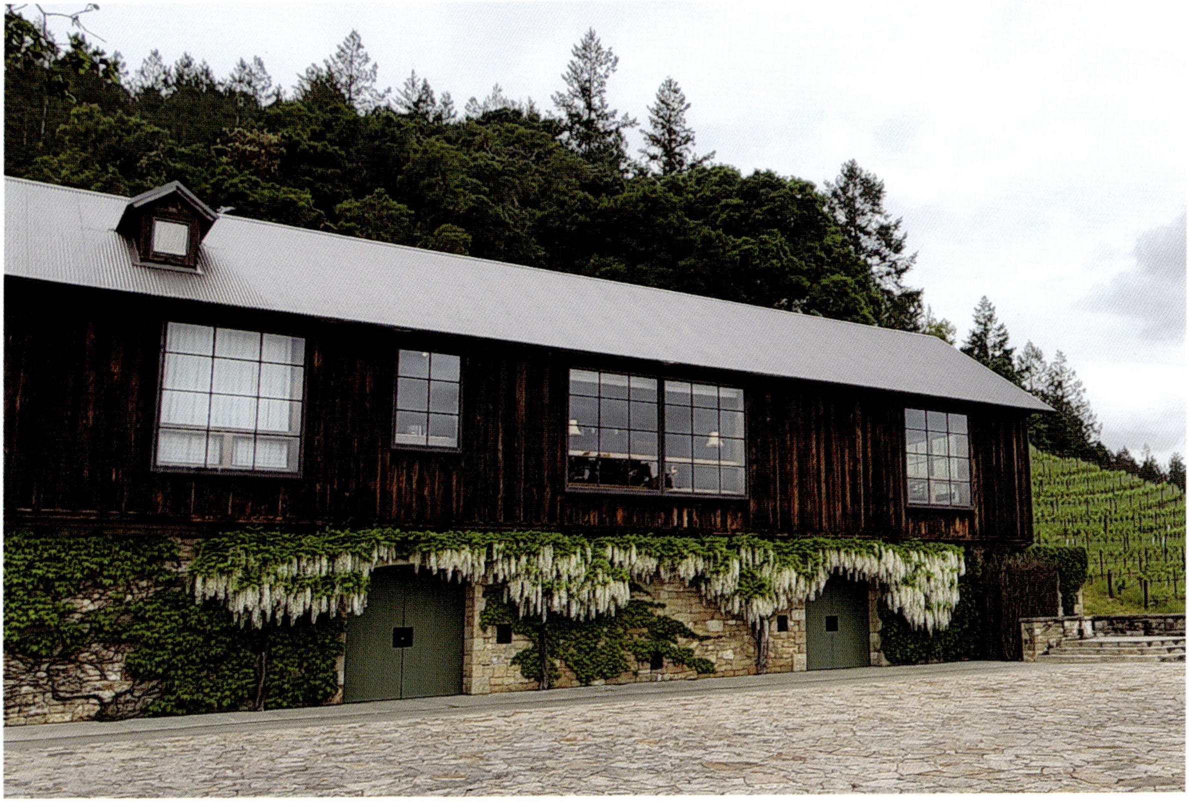

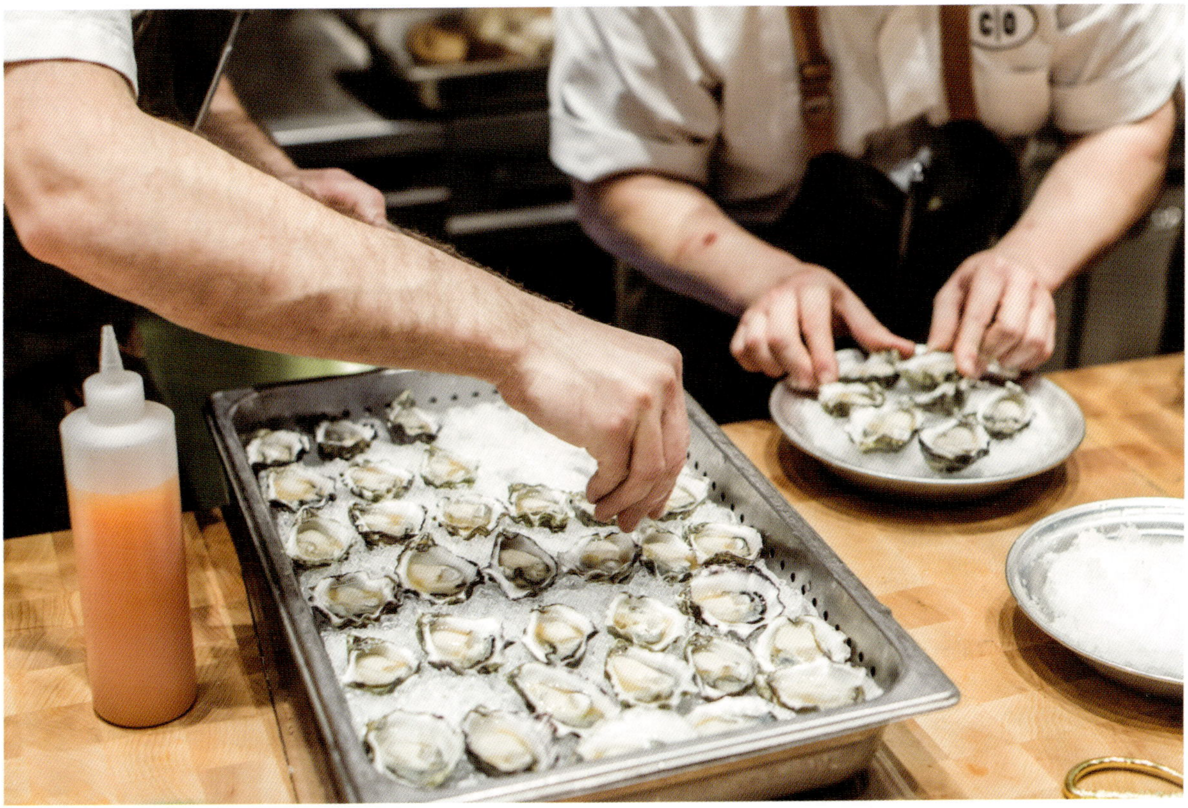

STRATEGIZE

"Stay really curious. Fall in love with the discovery process. Riff here, riff there—just like a musician does. You may only have twelve notes, but connect those notes in a fresh way. See what new direction you can bend something."

—DANNY MEYER, CEO IN RESTAURANT HOSPITALITY, SHAKE SHACK FOUNDER, *NEW YORK TIMES* BESTSELLING AUTHOR

Relationships take a lot of intentional strategy. They are *worth* a lot of strategy. And trust is going to develop between a few key relationships that will then influence on a larger scale.

Sometimes it's tempting for us to slide into autopilot and recreate a prior moment that mattered, but tailoring all aspects of the experience to fit a new person or new team is a critical part of what we do. And it's something we can all do, no matter what position we hold or what business we're in. Even if you're not hosting an event, you're always hosting a relationship. And you know which ones matter most.

"We keep detailed notes and make them accessible to everyone on the team. As soon as we find something out, we're writing it down: *he drinks Fiji water, so next time put that in his hotel room. She loves competition and willingly tries new things. He's an introvert and needs long spans of time for conversation. She's an early riser. He's never been to the Australian Open, but it would be a dream come true.*"

—STAN SMITH EVENTS TEAM

STRATEGIZE

#3 CHOOSE THE HOOK

The hook is what gets the "yes" to an invitation. It's giving someone unique access to a special location, event, experience, or person. People want to do what they want to do, and they're busy. If you're not offering something that excites them or opens access to something they care about or that they've always wanted to attend, they will likely turn it down (or cancel later on). A hook is not just about high-dollar experiences. We've had many clients tell us that it wasn't that their guests couldn't afford a certain ticket or meal at a specific restaurant, it's that it was never offered as a gifted experience and was often outside their normal way of life—even though it became exactly what they wanted.

Michael Anthony is the executive chef of Gramercy Tavern in New York City. We've been working with Michael, and Danny Meyer (who founded Union Square Hospitality Group), for years. Danny, Michael, and their teammates have beautifully created differentiation in the sea of restaurant sameness and trends in New York City, maintaining a consistent draw to Gramercy Tavern for thirty-plus years. It's one of our favorite partnerships and friendships, and bringing our friends and clients through the doors of a beloved and famous restaurant makes all of us happy. But beyond the thrill of a great meal and access to special moments within the restaurant itself, our vision for delighting our guests dovetails with Michael and Danny's.

We love how Michael describes the way they create both comfort and a powerful hook in a restaurant setting:

"We want our guests to be able to pronounce what's on the menu. It shouldn't feel strange or unidentifiable; our dishes should feel 'known' and comfortable. But you also need a great hook. Something that compels them to order it and choose our restaurant the next time. If the menu is too simple and plain, it's just boring. No one's going to tell their friends or family about a boring thing. We want them to sit down and say, 'Ah, I see exactly what's in front of me, I can identify this, but it's also exactly what I've been dreaming of.'"

—MICHAEL ANTHONY, JAMES BEARD AWARD WINNER AND AUTHOR

"Give them something they can't get anywhere else." —DAVIS LOVE III

STRATEGIZE

As you strategize about the right hook to get your "yes," think about that balance: a piece of it is familiar enough to make the recipient feel comfortable, but there's also something in the experience that will blow them away.

Sometimes a hook is an invitation to a renowned golf course, a private tour of a vineyard, a ticket to an exclusive event. But sometimes a hook is about giving space for a meaningful relationship to breathe in a wonderful setting: so you extend the invitation to their children as well, or a significant other, or a dear friend. You exceed their expectations in two directions.

Our world of high-end events has unique access points because of our relationships with partners and talent, and also the clients we serve and their budgets. However, think creatively about what you have access to—and how it's quite possible that it's a sparkling invitation to someone else.

WAYS TO CREATE A HOOK WITH UNIQUE ACCESS:
LINE UP CONVERSATIONS WITH AN EXPERT IN THEIR FIELD.
INVITE THEM TO SIT NEXT TO A ROLE MODEL.
COORDINATE A BEHIND-THE-SCENES TOUR OF A PLACE THEY LOVE.
UPGRADE THEIR TICKET.
CONNECT THEM TO SOMEONE THEY'VE ALWAYS WANTED TO MEET.
RESERVE A TABLE AT A BELOVED RESTAURANT.
INVITE THEM TO YOUR HOME.

"I love envisioning how to make SERVE come to life—and creating the right hook that will get our client to a 'wow.' My dad told me once that it wasn't my athletic talent that made me stand out (in my family), it was my competitive nature. And this continually drives me to win in an entrepreneurial way. So I think when you're trying to find the right hook, you need to think like an entrepreneur, a high-energy creative. Don't let things go flat or ordinary. Ordinary doesn't win." —GARY NIEBUR

"Frankly, going into Stan's closet will always be my favorite memory from the events we've done together. It was so personal and special. That weekend, we had incredible content: Venus Williams was with us, the resort was phenomenal, it was first class all the way. But years later, when I talk about that weekend with my company and our guests, the thing we talk about most is being invited to eat dinner with Stan and Margie at their family home. Then the pinnacle: Stan asked if we wanted to see his shoe collection, so we all squeezed into his closet. I have a photograph with my boss there, Stan's shoe collection all around us, and it's just one of those things that your brain can't quite compute. You can't believe you get access to such an intimate space. The vulnerability of that made a huge impression on all of us." —ED OLEBE

We choose a hook that will help get a "yes" to an invitation, but along the way, we've also had access open spontaneously during an event itself—like when we brought Nadia Comaneci and Bart Conner as the athletic talent to speak and be part of our client's Olympic Hospitality Program. Nadia and Bart are wonderful with guests, interactive and kind. What we didn't expect is that they would also join our guests in the seats and engage in casual conversation about the other athletes and happenings in front of us. They shared their expert knowledge, answered questions, joked around… and our guests loved it. To get side-by-side with a pro, in any field, and have intimate conversation is bucket-list material. With Nadia and Bart, it created a moment that mattered. Our clients and their guests had that access because we've spent years engaging in relationships and doing our best to take care of people. In turn, people want to take care of us.

You don't have to have access to Olympic medalists. We've watched leaders pair experienced employees with newly-promoted ones. Before the handoff, they've said things like, "We thought you may want to hear how she managed this or that…we thought you two would have much to talk about." **A simple, thoughtful gift of access like this—creating access between generations or levels of leadership—honors both sides.** It shows you're paying attention to who's in front of you, what might benefit those involved (with no benefit to yourself), and all it took was one intentional but quick interaction.

WHAT ARE SOME PLACES, PEOPLE, AND EXPERIENCES YOU HAVE ACCESS TO?

"As the restaurant world culture has grown over the last years, people are yearning for connection to it. There's the sensationalism around it for sure, like seeing the 'pirate ship' in real life, but I think it's also because people want to see full circle how we go from raw ingredients to what they'll experience on the table. When they watch our staff in the kitchen—even if just for a few minutes—there's definitely an astounding feeling of talent, coordination, professionalism. That peek behind the curtain creates a moment of revelation."

—MICHAEL ANTHONY

STRATEGIZE

So strategize hooks and access with creativity. Think outside the box and really cater to the uniqueness of your guest with the places, experiences, and people you can offer. Put yourself in their shoes, then imagine what shoes would be amazing to slide into. (We have one suggestion, and it's not Nikes.)

"When we've hosted events with Stan and Gary, we invite VIPs, but we also invite the next level coming from behind. It gives them access to our most valued relationships that they wouldn't have otherwise, giving them a sense of gravitas and building a foundation for their forward movement." —TRACEY BOWRA

FLIP BACK TO PAGE 35, WHERE YOU NAMED SOMEONE'S TRUST YOU WANT TO WIN OR DEEPEN THIS YEAR. WHAT IS A HOOK YOU COULD OFFER THAT PERSON, TO INVITE THEM INTO AN ENGAGING EXPERIENCE WITH YOU?

"What Maya Angelou said is very true: People won't remember what you said. They won't remember what you did. But they will remember how you made them feel."

—DANIELLE VINCENT, FORTUNE 500 SENIOR VP HEAD OF RETAIL CARD SERVICES

ENGAGE:
OPEN HEARTS

Care about and engage with the whole person—not just the transaction or business deal—so each client and guest feels known, valued, and comfortable in any given situation.

CREATING MOMENTS THAT MATTER to form relational bonds is an extremely valuable tool. Meaningful interactions lead to meaningful results. Sometimes the results show up quickly, like an enthusiastic new partnership or a business deal with a sought-after client. Sometimes the results show up unexpectedly when something goes south and you're met with forgiveness and grace because you've already established a relationship that's deemed valuable on both sides. Sometimes the results of these meaningful moments show up a few years down the road, but you can point back to when you stepped outside the normal routine or status quo and more fully engaged and connected: human to human, heart to heart, life to life.

When you've put a meaningful and strategic plan in place, with a compelling hook or two, now you've set up the possibility to really engage and be present with the people around you during the experience itself. You've designed the macromoment. Now you're in position to build momentum throughout the event with highly engaged micromoments.

The best host is the host who's genuinely paying attention to his or her guests. But sometimes engaging with the hearts of other people takes a bit of training and a few tips, especially if we're out of practice. We understand it's a moment that matters, and we've designed a specific event around it, but often we need some help once we're in the midst of the moment. So we've compiled our favorite tips: **serve outside of your role for the win-win, model vulnerability, and redirect the spotlight.**

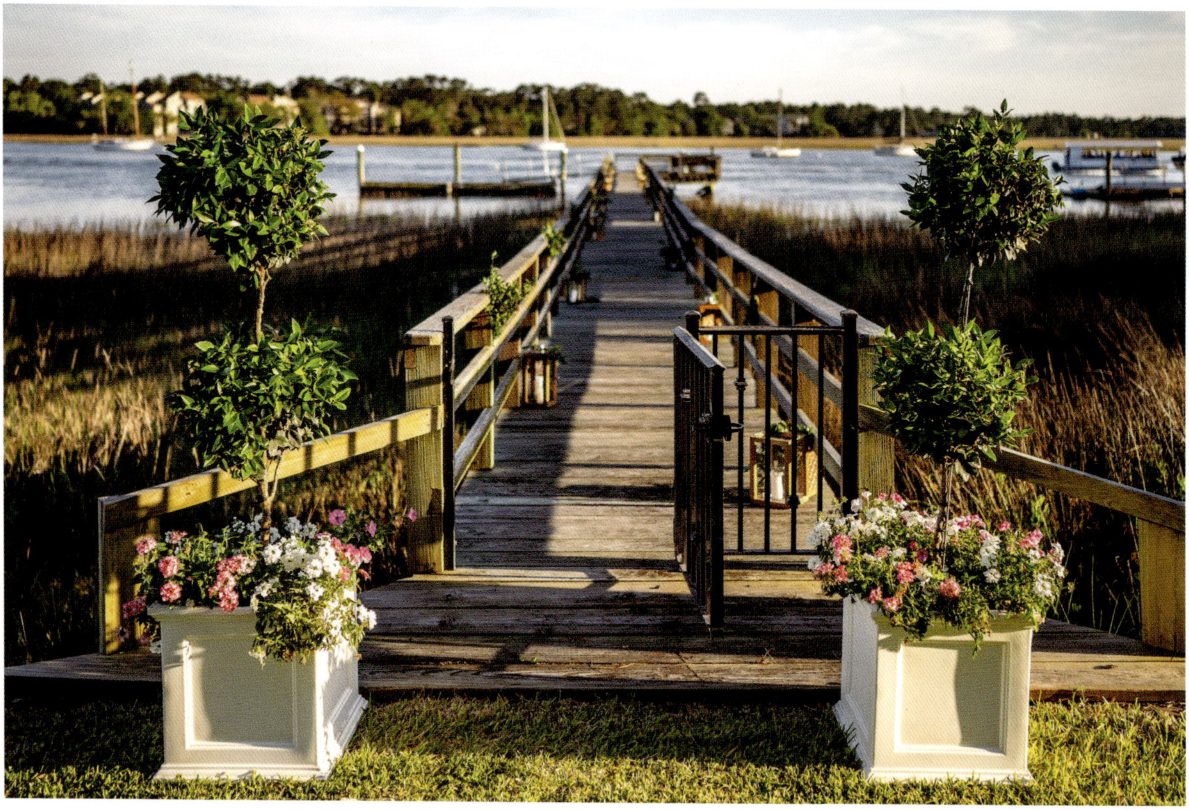

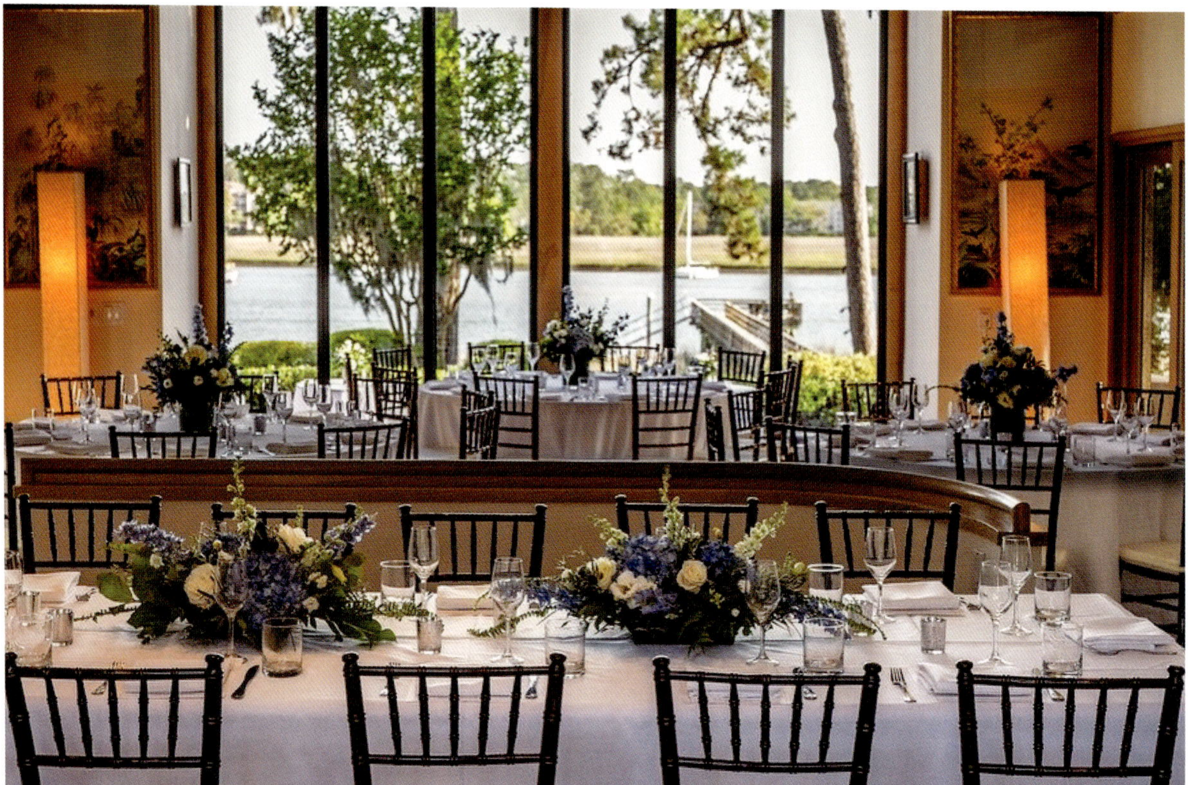

"What I witnessed with Stan Smith Events, through both Gary and Stan, is a genuine interest in the people in the room. They sit down with guests and engage in broader conversations outside of any preset chats and speeches. It's an overwhelming down-to-earth feeling with these guys. They give time to deepen relationships—and ultimately the guest's experience. Seeing this engagement showed me our values were aligned, and I trusted them to represent what our company stands for."

—STUART IRVING, PRESIDENT AND CEO, FINANCIAL SERVICES

#1 SERVE OUTSIDE THE LINES

Davis Love III is the winner of twenty-one events on the PGA Tour. He won a PGA Championship and carries medals and high rankings from one course to the next. He was always a leader while playing on the tour, so he was a popular pick as captain for the 2012 US Ryder Cup Team. But we've seen that it's the way Davis serves outside his role—outside the lines of expectation—that creates highly engaged and trusting relationships.

> "Davis builds trust horizontally. He models care, human to human, by doing simple and sometimes menial tasks that go outside of his role… because he actually sees it as his role. This kind of serving is humble, team-unifying, and critical when you're building cohesiveness and trust." —STAN SMITH

During his captaincy, Davis did things like get up in the middle of the night to pick up a player from the airport, carry their bags, charge golf carts, clean players' clubs. He didn't elevate his own status over the purpose of what he set out to do—which was to create a winning team. So he led his players by giving them all the space they needed to focus on their game. And in those small but significant moments of serving them, he earned their trust. They knew he was there to prepare them to win, and he would serve outside the lines to get them there.

Here's where the story takes an interesting turn. His team didn't win.

"After we lost the 2012 Ryder Cup, we got around the table as players, coaches, and staff. We had made some bad decisions. I had made some. So I told them honestly where I thought I had screwed up. I asked for both advice and criticism. They agreed that I had made some mistakes, and I owned it. I'll never forget how at the end of that process, they began listing all the things that make a great captain, and what would make a great team for the next twenty years. Then they said, 'Davis, you're the captain.' I couldn't believe it. But I think when you show you're part of the team, and you're willing to work toward a solution, you build trust. To have a group of players and future captains trust in what you can do… that was an unbelievable moment for me."

—DAVIS LOVE III

"You earn your team's trust because you're giving them the opportunity to succeed, and they can feel that. They see you'll do whatever it takes to take care of them." —DAVIS LOVE III

Then in 2016, his team won the Ryder Cup.

Davis engaged to win trust in two powerful ways: as a leader, he served outside his role. And then with that same humility, he owned what he needed to own. He admitted where he failed and dug into problem-solving, even though he had zero expectation that he would ever captain that team again. Whether or not he was captain, he wanted their win.

Taking a humble position will engage hearts. Taking ownership of where you mess up, and being open to hearing advice and criticism, invites those who are following you to do the same. When you set this tone, it creates the space to be vulnerable, and as we'll see in the next section, vulnerability is the birthplace of lasting relationships.

HOW COULD YOU SERVE OUTSIDE YOUR LINES THIS WEEK?
WHOM COULD YOU SERVE?

#2 MODEL VULNERABILITY

It was an idyllic day in Napa Valley. Our client and their guests had flown in from all over the country to spend a few days together. These were leaders who represented massive companies and were looking for someone who could turn an environment from surface-level, business-heavy conversation to something more meaningful.

After months of team planning—and figuring out what hooks and access would delight guests, like we described in the strategize chapter—we landed on hosting a phenomenal meal at The French Laundry and a private, retreat-like space for fireside chats. Then we opened the doors to Hugh Jackman. While Hugh is certainly beloved by the millions who have watched his acting and producing career shine, we also invited Hugh for another reason.

When we started SSE, we had already seen a few speakers flop. We watched as event teams hired famous talent, and after the initial jaw-drop of getting to meet a legend, the legend was so focused on their own story and fame that what was meant to be a gift to the guests actually turned into an ego show. Not only was it off-putting, but it also created a formal barrier between speaker and guest. There was no exchange, no connection. We wanted to steer as clear of that as possible. Yes, it's always thrilling to meet someone who's famous, but if there's not a level of generosity and vulnerability coming from the front of the room, the heart of the guests will not open. The crowd may be impressed and starstruck, but they won't feel at ease. They won't be moved. This is why strategizing to choose the right hook is so valuable, because you're considering the whole person and how the event will unfold—not just blindly throwing shiny objects in front of people.

ENGAGE

"Memorable moments have a crescendo effect."

—GARY NIEBUR

So after our guests got photographs with Hugh, we closed the doors behind us. We told our guests we weren't broadcasting any of this (all phones and recording devices went away), and we said, "This is a time for you to meet Hugh, hear from his heart, and ask him questions." So of course we won't broadcast details here in this book, because this is a huge part of why this SERVE model works and trust is built: you create a safe space for hearts to be opened. If people are anxious, or walking on eggshells, or think they're part of some performance or status check—their guard will most likely stay high.

This isn't what happened in Napa. Hugh opened up graciously and generously, in part because our client for that event got up with him and asked him questions while modeling his own vulnerability. Because our client took this vulnerable direction, so did Hugh, and so did our guests.

One specific guest, who was carrying a heavy but personal burden, felt the freedom to ask Hugh how he handled it when something pivotal that he was counting on did not, in fact, unfold. It was a tender scene to watch. Hugh shared about the backstory of making the movie *The Greatest Showman*, and how a huge investor backed out during production, and suddenly Hugh was faced with either pulling the plug or picking up the pieces and trusting his way forward on his own dime. In that moment, *The Greatest Showman* was not a showman at all: he was a human responding to a human.

We will never know the full effect of that fireside conversation, because so much of this trust work is also about the intangible and long view, but we put our money on its impact. Our guest walked away feeling valued, understood, and helped in a personal way. Our client walked away realizing that his vulnerability opened doors that he couldn't have known needed to open. And we hope Hugh walked away knowing that his vulnerability opened hearts, and it was well worth doing.

Who are *you* putting in front of your people? Who stands in front of the room and sets the tone? Who are you, in front of your people? Whether it's a leadership summit, a church conference, a family dinner… if you want to engage people's hearts and accelerate trust, your chances of that happening are greatly turned up if you lead with openness and vulnerability. In other words, be honest and admit a fault once in a while, admit what you're really feeling or experiencing. Because in the end, no one trusts a showman. And since we all know that no human is capable of perfection, it's a reminder that we're not alone. We break the wall of pretend formality and the pedestal effect.

ENGAGE

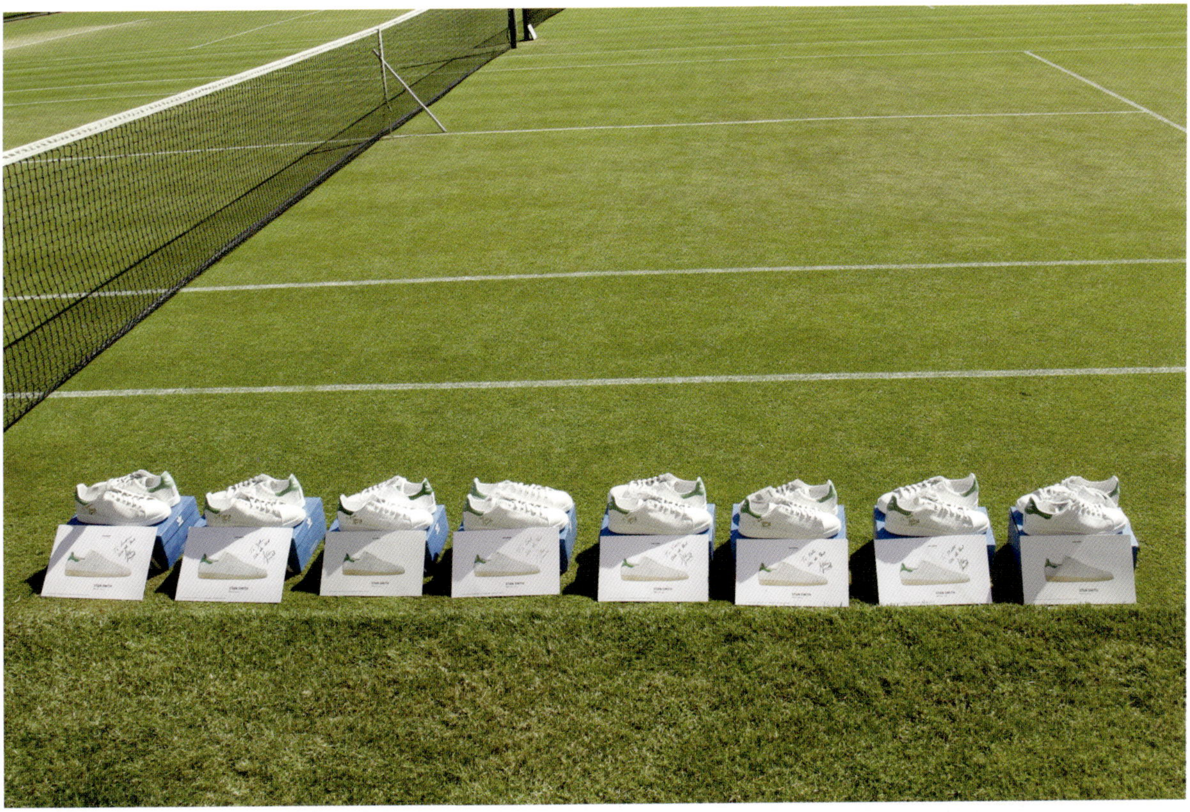

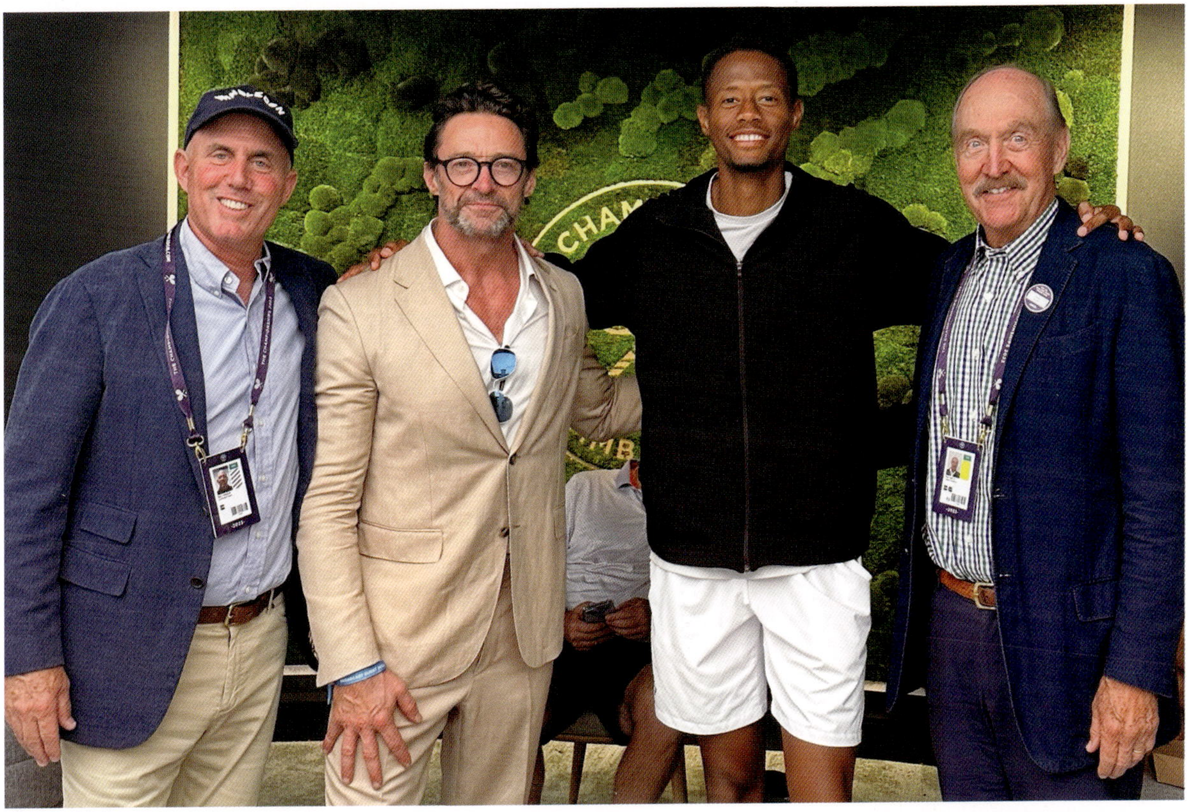

"Usually trust is earned over a long period of time with consistency and doing what we say we'll do, following through, sharing, caring. That's the natural way. But when you need to accelerate trust, vulnerability is a huge piece. It's like exposing your flank—being the first one to open up, whether that be for a team, an individual, or an organization. I'm a more guarded person, an introvert, so this wasn't natural at first. But it was modeled to me eight years ago, and I've been doing it ever since, and it has worked over and over again. Usually it's some version of getting up in front of people, whether 5 or 500, and sharing something personal with emotional transparency. It doesn't have to be a traumatic thing, just something meaningful that moves you. It gives people a chance to see a genuine human being in front of them. They suddenly see you as someone with hopes, fears, concerns, problems. Sometimes it overwhelms me…literally I've had to stop for a minute to compose myself because I was talking about my kids or a parent. But what it builds is a desire to reciprocate. The human reaction to someone being vulnerable is you want to do the same thing back. People will try to find something, usually, that's roughly equal to what you shared. This helps us get over some of the natural human defenses we put up, because of course we all have some armor to keep ourselves sane. But you can't connect until you let that guard down a little bit. In all of my experience, when I've put down my shield, the other person has too." —ED OLEBE

"Don't have a veneer. If you have to come to work and play-act, it's not going to be worth it. People don't trust people who are one person in one setting, another person somewhere else. Be the same everywhere."

—STEVE SQUERI, FORTUNE 100 CEO

In 2020, we watched as another one of our clients was vulnerable in a way that had a deep impact on his most valued customers. As the CEO of a major airline, Ed Bastian leveraged trusted relationships at a time when the climate of fear and chaos typically shuts down engagement and vulnerability—because he did the opposite.

In the harrowing first few weeks and months of COVID, as the world was shutting down rapidly, people were afraid for their health and their livelihood. People's ability to do business, to see loved ones, to even get home from faraway places was at stake. Equally, the future of airlines was at risk.

In a period of crisis, the tendency is to avoid making statements until PR, legal, operations, customer service—all departments are sure and clear of any ramification. Every word and action is considered and vetted. But this was an unprecedented level of crisis for both the airline and the traveler. There wasn't time to ensure every interest was fully vetted. Ed chose to step into the moment with direct engagement, a vulnerable tone, and a compassionate focus that reflected he understood what was at stake.

In what was later lauded by many as an exceptional demonstration of vulnerable leadership, Ed sent a very transparent and vulnerable email to all their loyalty members on March 15, 2020, just four days after WHO had declared COVID-19 as a global pandemic and before most companies had fully shut down all travel.

The email opens with deep care, concern, and commitment to the traveler:

> *"We are in unprecedented times. With the ongoing spread of COVID-19 (coronavirus) and the incredible speed at which things are changing around us, we are continually adapting our operations and business. With recent reductions in our flight schedule, I personally want to ensure that every member of our Delta family is informed on an ongoing basis, including you.*
>
> *As an airline, we have faced many challenges, and each has made us better prepared for a situation like this. Caring for you continues to be our top priority, and our people are working tirelessly across the globe, taking every precaution to make sure that when you are ready to travel, Delta is here for you.*
>
> *We are working around the clock to:*
> *Protect you and your loved ones when you fly. You have my promise that our team is going above and beyond the guidance of the Centers for Disease Control and Prevention and the World Health Organization to ensure your safety. We are building on an ever-present focus on cleanliness and continually assessing ways to enhance your safety throughout the travel experience."*—Ed Bastian, CEO airline industry

Five times throughout the email Ed uses the first-person pronoun, stepping as CEO directly into the conversation, affirming his commitment to what his customers cared most about in those unnerving moments.

He would go on to send six more emails throughout 2020, each time being vulnerable—each time expressing commitment to the flier, each time taking action that backed up those commitments—from extending flier status, to rolling over miles, to taking the extraordinary step to block middle seats, creating a psychological sense of safety for fliers. Taking a step that presumably cost them money actually created a deeper sense of loyalty. Remarkably, in addition to his customer emails, Ed sent a total of 46 memos to employees that year, averaging one a week once the pandemic began. Those memos had the same tone of transparency and vulnerability that Ed displayed with his customers. This kind of posture is the heart of Engage—a deep commitment to others' best.

ENGAGE

ENGAGE

"Vulnerability invites vulnerability, and in this space, trust can be born."

—GARY NIEBUR

GET YOUR TEAM OR FAMILY TOGETHER AND SHARE SOMETHING WITH TRANSPARENCY AND VULNERABILITY. ASK OTHERS IF THEY'VE EVER HAD A SIMILAR EXPERIENCE OR FELT THE SAME WAY, AND SEE IF IT OPENS DOORS. (IF IT DOESN'T AT FIRST, DON'T COUNT IT A FAILURE. TRY AGAIN IN A COUPLE WEEKS. GIVE PEOPLE A CHANCE TO OPEN UP AND FEEL SAFE TOO.)

#3 REDIRECT THE SPOTLIGHT

When you're creating moments that matter, you're creating them for someone else. Even if we have an objective that will also benefit others, and maybe that's just someday down the road, we are still creating these experiences because a person matters. Leaning into humility and nudging others into the spotlight, in whatever form that takes, is another great way to engage hearts and show that you value who they are and what they do.

People love to be loved.

When we host an event with a client, we try to direct the spotlight onto others, and our partners and talent do the same. Because if our client gets all the glory for whatever meaningful moments come out of doing an event with us, then we've done our job well. Whether it's a client to their customer or how we treat our families, we should ultimately exist to elevate and SERVE others.

If people are going to feel special, then we need to show them they are special by how we engage with them—and this comes from believing in every human's worth in the first place. Sometimes it's easy to direct the spotlight on someone and show our belief in their value because they hit the same marks we value and also treat others well. We naturally want to praise these sorts of people and shine the spotlight on them. Other times it's much more difficult. When it's difficult, get to know that person better. Ask good questions about many different areas of their life; believe in how multifaceted every person is, and it will help break through any flattened caricature or reputation you may carry. Find something (and you will!) to call out, to praise, to honor.

"The first event we did with you guys, we were just a growth start-up. We had a location, a kinda cool business, and an affinity for each other. But what happened for that event is that you guys came in and Stan did this judo move: all of a sudden he made us the talent. He flipped the script."

—SID MASHBURN, AMERICAN FASHION DESIGNER AND HEAD OF MASHBURN BRAND

"You made us the showcase! You made us look elevated and fantastic. It was a halo effect…because we were associated with you. You lifted us up."

—ANN MASHBURN, AMERICAN FASHION DESIGNER AND HEAD OF MASHBURN BRAND

"I learned so much about every human's value from my parents. My dad took a second job as a supervisor of a department store to help support our family, and I was working in the same place stocking shelves, so I got to watch my dad as a leader. There was a group of young managers in the training program who my dad had to supervise, and they were just horrible and snotty. I couldn't believe how well my dad still treated them, and when I asked him about it, he said, 'You have to treat people how you want to be treated…even if they don't treat you well. One day, they may learn.'"

—STEVE SQUERI

ENGAGE

We all have the chance to engage and open hearts—all sorts of hearts. The payoff is immense, whether it's happening in the business world or your family circle, whether it's people you've just met and are investing in or those who have been in your circle for years and still need that experience of being engaged, prized, and valued.

CONSIDER A FEW PEOPLE (OR GROUPS OF PEOPLE) WHOSE HEARTS YOU WANT TO OPEN THIS YEAR. FOR EACH ONE, ANSWER THE FOLLOWING QUESTIONS:

WHAT DO YOU WANT THEM TO FEEL?

HOW COULD YOU SHOW OR COMMUNICATE THEIR VALUE?

WHEN COULD YOU REDIRECT THE SPOTLIGHT—AND HOW WILL YOU DO IT?

I've been a guest of some incredible events, but there's a common pattern how events are done. The first time I was invited to a Stan Smith Event, I felt the uncommonness of what they do. It was very personal. We weren't just being entertained—Stan, Gary, and their team have this way of reaching over the net and engaging the people around them. They make each person feel welcomed and valued. They know everyone's name; they ask questions about your life. We were at Wimbledon, and with their expertise, they brought us into the tennis world by caring that we understood what was happening. So in the end, you really feel part of things. And when my own company hired Stan Smith Events and we brought guests, I saw how Stan Smith Events and their nature rubbed off on us. We engaged authentically with our guests, just as they were doing. And after those few days of connection, recreating, learning about one another, truly enjoying the experience—we won friendship, won trust, won business. It wasn't transactional. It's a human approach, and I think that's what sets Stan Smith Events apart. They care about people and model it, so you walk away doing the same."

—JOHN SLAMECKA, FORTUNE 100 PRESIDENT

ENGAGE

"A lot of vendors plan good events. But what sets Stan Smith Events apart is how affable, warm, and friendly they are…and how their attention to our guests is the best I've seen. It permeates everything they do. They both make our guests feel special and give them an experience they've never had before. I've watched them do this for years. They create the best client entertainment events I've attended."

—STEVE SQUERI

THE NEXT TIME YOU'RE WITH THE PERSON OR GROUP YOU'RE WANTING TO ENGAGE THIS YEAR, ASK A QUESTION THAT STIRS NEW CONNECTION. HERE ARE A FEW TO SPARK YOUR OWN IDEAS:

"WHO HAS HAD THE GREATEST IMPACT ON YOUR LIFE?"

"HOW DID YOU MEET YOUR SPOUSE OR PARTNER?"

"WHAT'S A PLACE YOU'VE ALWAYS WANTED TO GO—AND WHAT DRAWS YOU TO IT?"

"WHAT'S ONE OF YOUR FAVORITE ACTIVITIES OR HOBBIES—AND HOW DID YOU GET INTRODUCED TO IT?"

"WHAT'S A LIFE DECISION THAT CHANGED THE DIRECTION YOU WERE HEADED?"

"WHAT'S ONE OF YOUR FAVORITE MEMORIES FROM THE PAST TEN YEARS?"

F

"Play is a hallmark of Stan Smith Events."

—DAVIS LOVE III

RECREATE:
PLAY TOGETHER

Build bonds and shared memories through fun experiences like team challenges and mini tournaments. Guards come down; trust grows.

MAYBE IT'S NOT A SURPRISE COMING FROM TWO TENNIS PLAYERS: *We love to play.* But we don't just love games and competitions because it's in our blood. We believe recreation is a significant piece of making moments that matter, which is why we're giving it a whole chapter and why it's a part of every experience we design at Stan Smith Events.

We've continually experienced recreation as a dynamic tool for accelerating trust and deepening relationships in a way that doesn't happen when we're all sitting behind desks or in the stands doing the same-old, same-old. We've seen how the spirit of play and a good dose of friendly competition really opens up space for people to let down their guard and feel more fully alive, even open sides of themselves that had been dormant. Leaders become more approachable and humanized. Clients and their guests bond over the lighthearted, shared memory. And even, quite often, the "games" skeptics turn into fans.

When we get client feedback after an event, whatever high-spirited games, tournaments, and closing moments we've set up are often right at the top of the list. Then sometimes we hear how those clients and guests have made it part of their family life too, as a way to bond with their children, or how they have brought play into the teams and sessions they lead as a way to break the ice or celebrate a win or get a team functioning in a more connected way.

"I remember my first Stan Smith Event was when I was a guest of one of your clients. It was a US Open event in New York City, and we all went to a Danny Meyer restaurant in Lower Manhattan—one with expansive, breathtaking views. So immediately you're bowled over. Then we had a great business session….Then I heard we were going to move into games. At first I was thinking, 'Games? We're doing games?' But within three minutes, I understood why. You get a room of type A individuals and put a game in front of them, and immediately they're rolling up their sleeves, strategizing with one another, trying to figure out how their team's gonna win this thing…when of course winning really doesn't matter. But I saw the whole thing work. You get people shooting baskets or playing cornhole, and for someone new on the scene like I was, I felt welcomed and included right away. I was quickly part of the group because games just naturally draw you together. Then for the rest of the weekend, you have that groundwork in place. You're all connected, engaged, energized." —ED OLEBE

RECREATE

RECREATE

We'll never cut recreation out. We'll weave it into our itinerary for every weekend event we host, even if sometimes we have to work hard to convince our clients that even some quick, playful activities and accolades can serve as intermission.

To be clear: we're not talking about high-stakes games. We're talking about cornhole, axe-throwing, glow-in-the-dark golf, wine tasting competition, ping-pong, horseshoes, go-karting, off-roading through a canyon. We throw tennis and golf in the mix too, but in a very all-level, friendly way. No one's out there trying to get a job promotion or beat Stan in a singles match (he won't let you).

We've seen recreating works best when it feels safe and inviting to all, even if it's outside of people's comfort zones, which means you'll have to convince at least half of your people that it's really, truly, honestly just about fun. To recreate in a way that creates memorable experiences, we hold to three things: **level the playing field, push through resistance, and mark the moment with awards…or champagne.**

CONSIDER A FEW GAMES OR ACTIVITIES YOU LOVE (EVEN IF IT'S BEEN A WHILE SINCE YOU'VE PLAYED THEM). INVITE SOMEONE TO JOIN YOU FOR ONE.

"Stan, Gary, and their team find a way for every single person to compete. Whether it's on a court, playing some form of trivia, making score predictions…they make sure every client and their guest is having a good time. And it's not fake or a check-the-box. They lean in all the way, and you can tell by how they enthusiastically include everyone that they love and care about what they're doing for others."

—KEVIN WARREN, FORMER FORTUNE 100 CMO

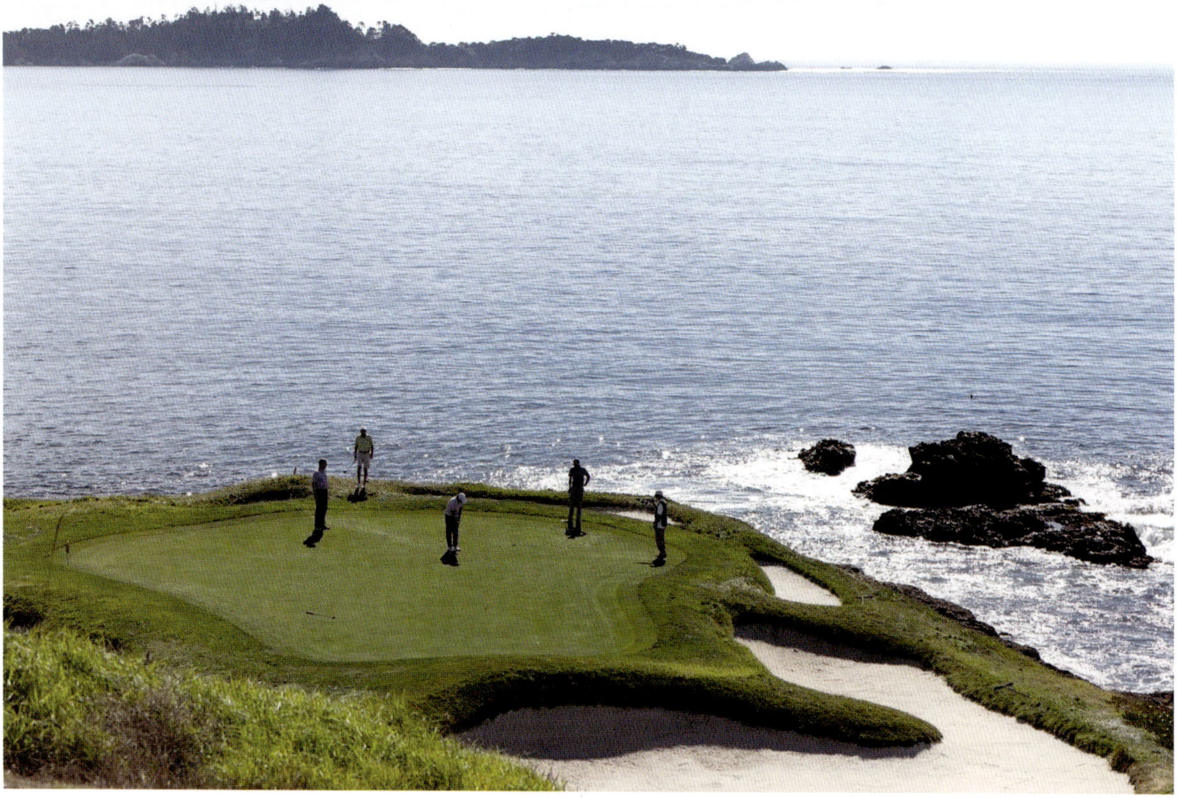

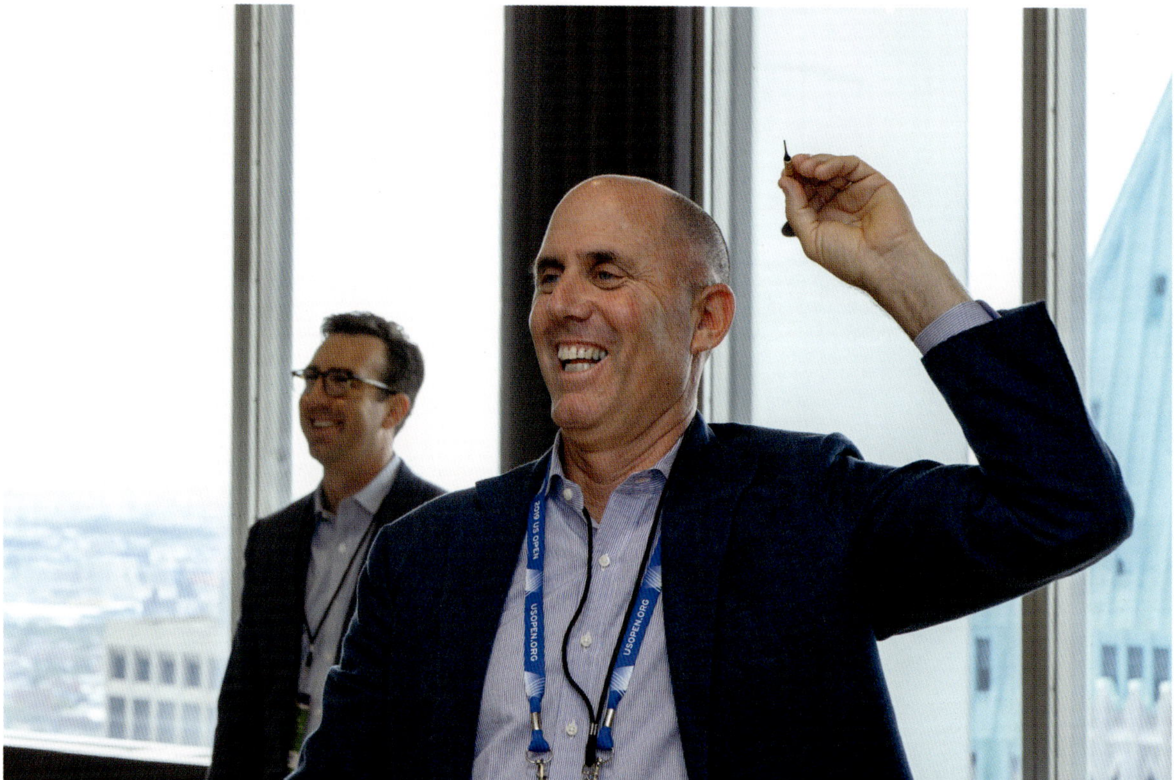
2019 US OPEN
USOPEN.ORG
USOPEN.ORG

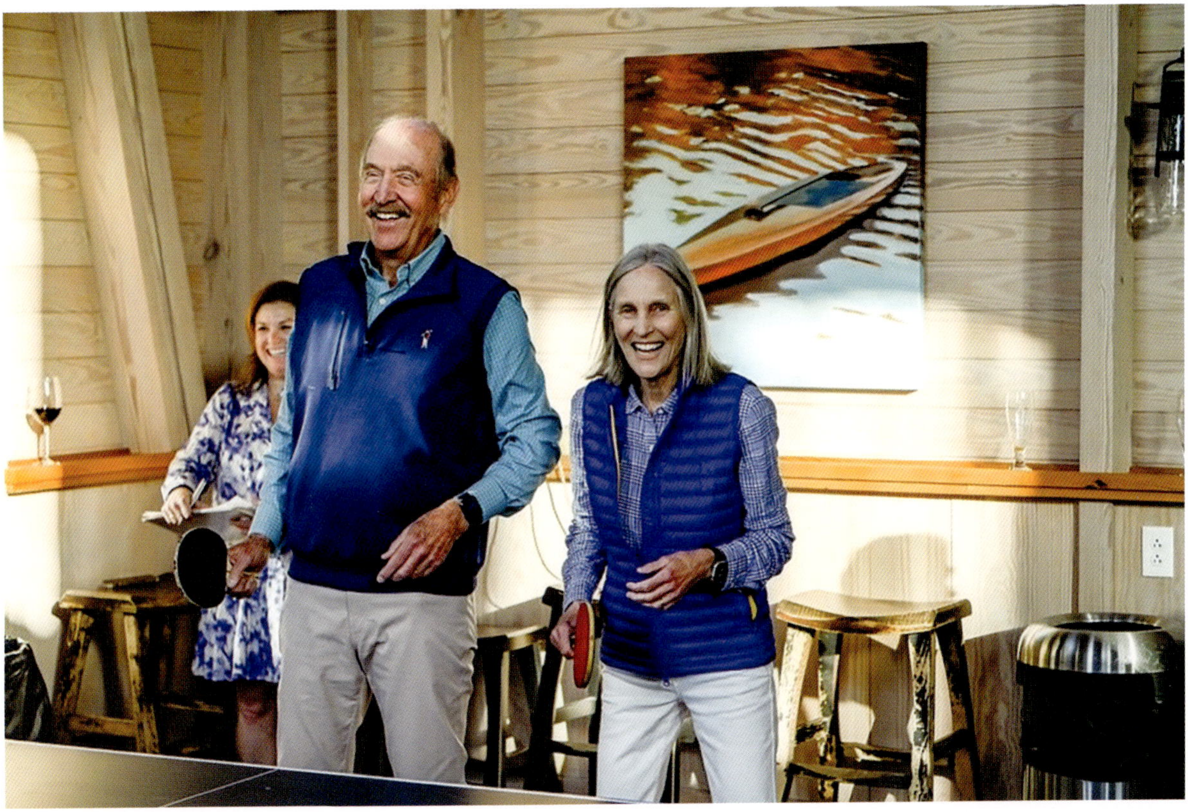

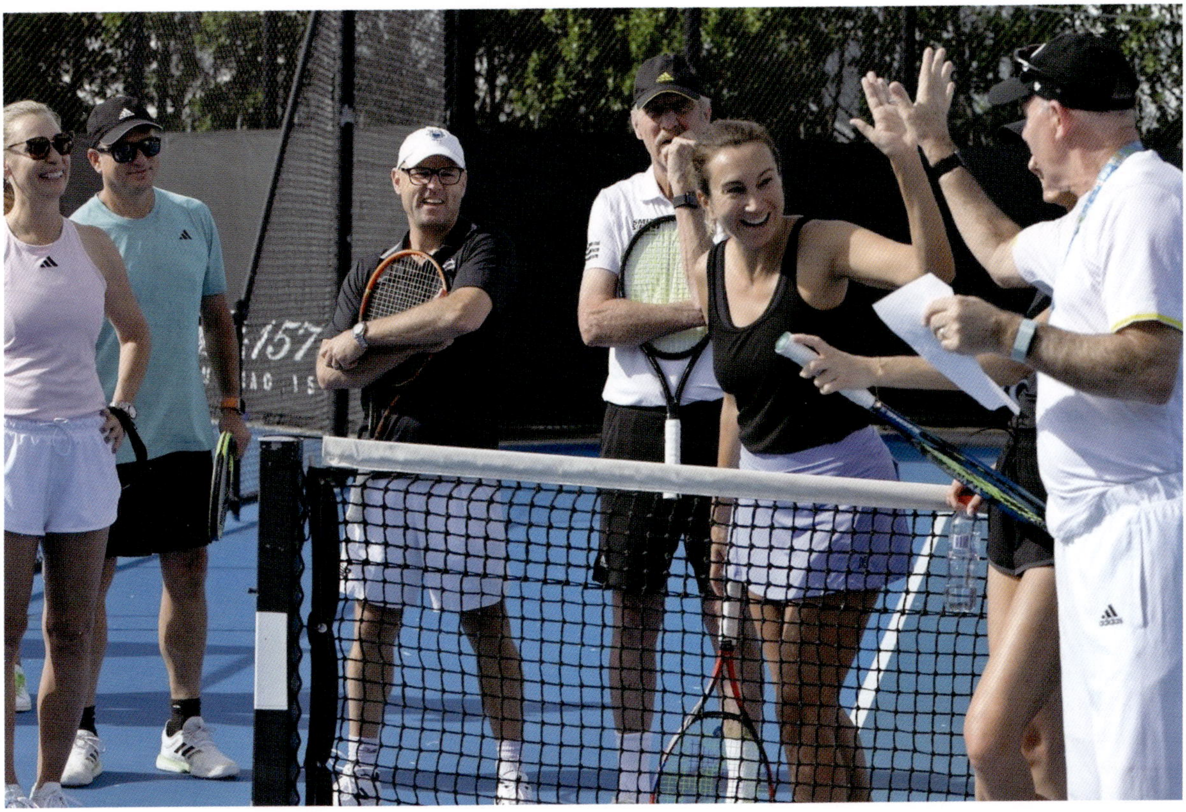
157

#1 LEVEL THE PLAYING FIELD

It can be difficult in the corporate world to get away from roles and who's who running what. Even in work cultures that are very open-door and invitational at high levels, it's a challenge to level the playing field in a tangible way. Or if you're trying to build trust between potential clients and partners, it can be a challenge to get people warmed up, laughing, and letting down their guard.

This is the magic of games. Anyone can win or lose. Anyone can turn into a star or a surprising pinch-hitter. A serious CEO could go nuts. A pro could whiff.

We definitely do what we can to level the playing field in recreation. If someone's really good at an activity we're doing, we'll make it more challenging for that person so it's a fair fight. If someone's fumbling along, we'll get next to that person and coach them into a great shot or winning toss. And we'll add in some easy, low-barrier activities too, like guessing who's going to win the match or predicting who's going to win the rugby game or which wine is top shelf.

WHO'S A GROUP YOU COULD BRING TOGETHER FOR A GAME?

WHAT'S A GAME OR SPORT YOU'VE NEVER—OR BARELY—PLAYED? (REMEMBER, THE GOAL IS TO LEVEL THE PLAYING FIELD.)

WHAT ARE SOME WAYS YOU CAN RECREATE WITH YOUR FAMILY, SPOUSE, OR SIGNIFICANT OTHER?

"Davis Love III and I still talk about the time we threw axes at an event in Virginia. Davis wasn't any good at it, and I wasn't really either, which I think was funny for our clients and guests. Davis got pretty intense trying to hit the target. Apparently there's still an ax lost in the woods somewhere." —STAN SMITH

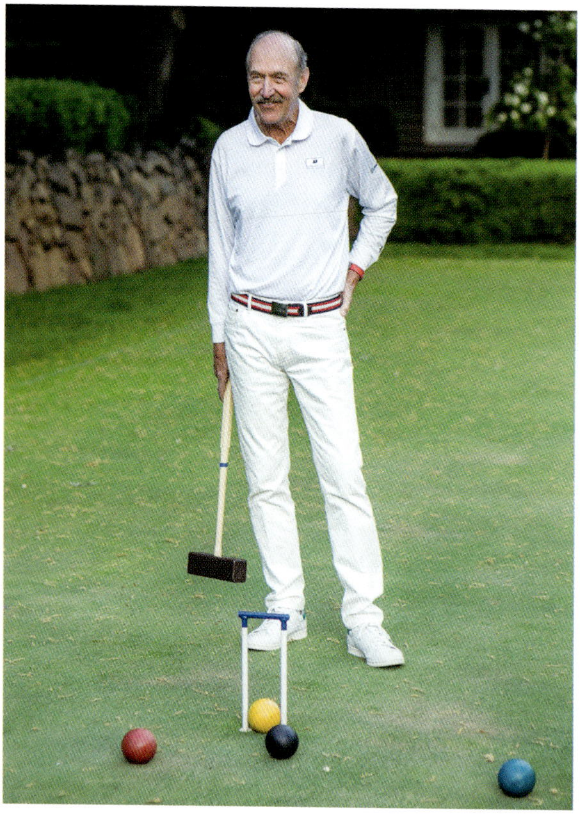
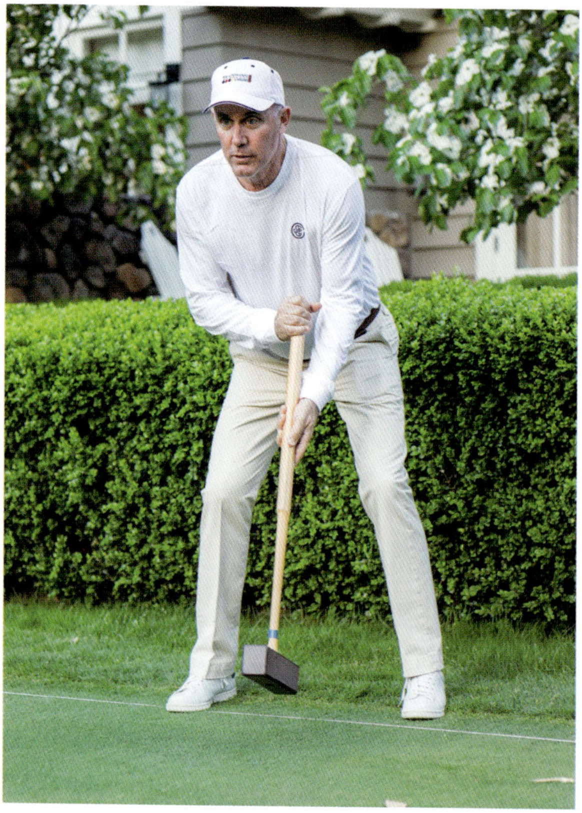
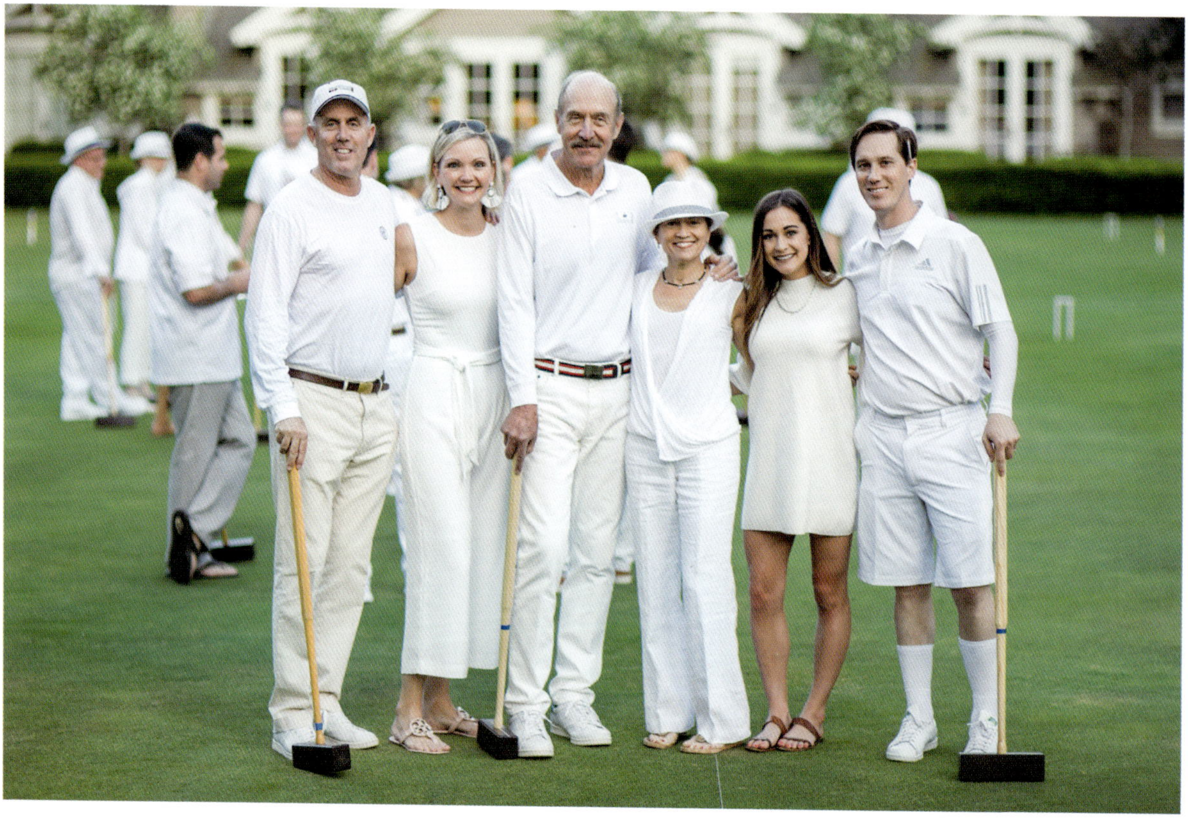

bardessono
Spring
WATER
Luongo
Color/appearance:
Nose:
Mouth:
Conclusion/rank:

"One of the things that stands out to me from our events together is when we brought in a former senator to speak, and he ended up sticking around for the whole weekend. We were playing some game with croquet balls, and…the playfulness of that game we were playing brought the walls down. It humanized everybody. Regardless of your position, whether you're the CEO or a power broker, we're all playing this game. Having fun. Being people. And once you get everyone on that same plane, now you can have those conversations. It's why things like this matter." —MICHAEL RITTLER

As hosts, we're also willing to look a bit ridiculous to make people laugh—which is a way of adding that engaging level of vulnerability *with* the power of play. It's funny to a crowd when a former tennis pro tries to get on a pommel horse and tries to do a routine after Nadia Comaneci and Bart Conner demonstrated their Olympic-gold level moves. Or when a boss gets in front of his employees and tries a game or sport she's never attempted, happy to entertain, no matter how poorly it goes. When a leader or person in front is willing to get over their own ego or self-concern, it's disarming and memorable in a big way, adding yet another layer to creating moments that matter.

Recently at one of our events we tried another way of leveling the playing field: we swapped out golf and tennis for pickleball. It was a game changer! Pickleball has become such a popular sport, and it's fairly easy to jump into it whether or not you've ever played, so our client loved the idea of trying it out. For that weekend, we brought in Kim Clijsters, a former tennis pro who was the first Belgian player to reach the world No. 1 ranking, as well as champion of all four Grand Slam tournaments.

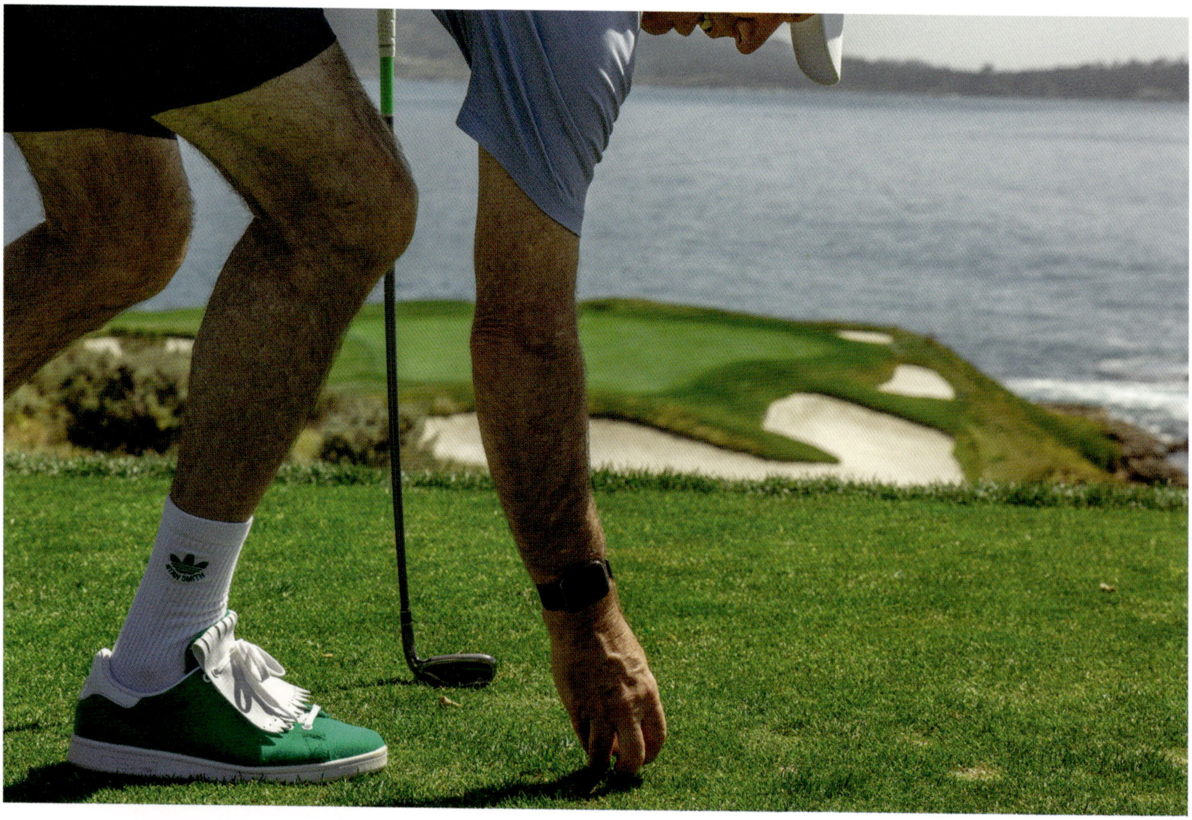

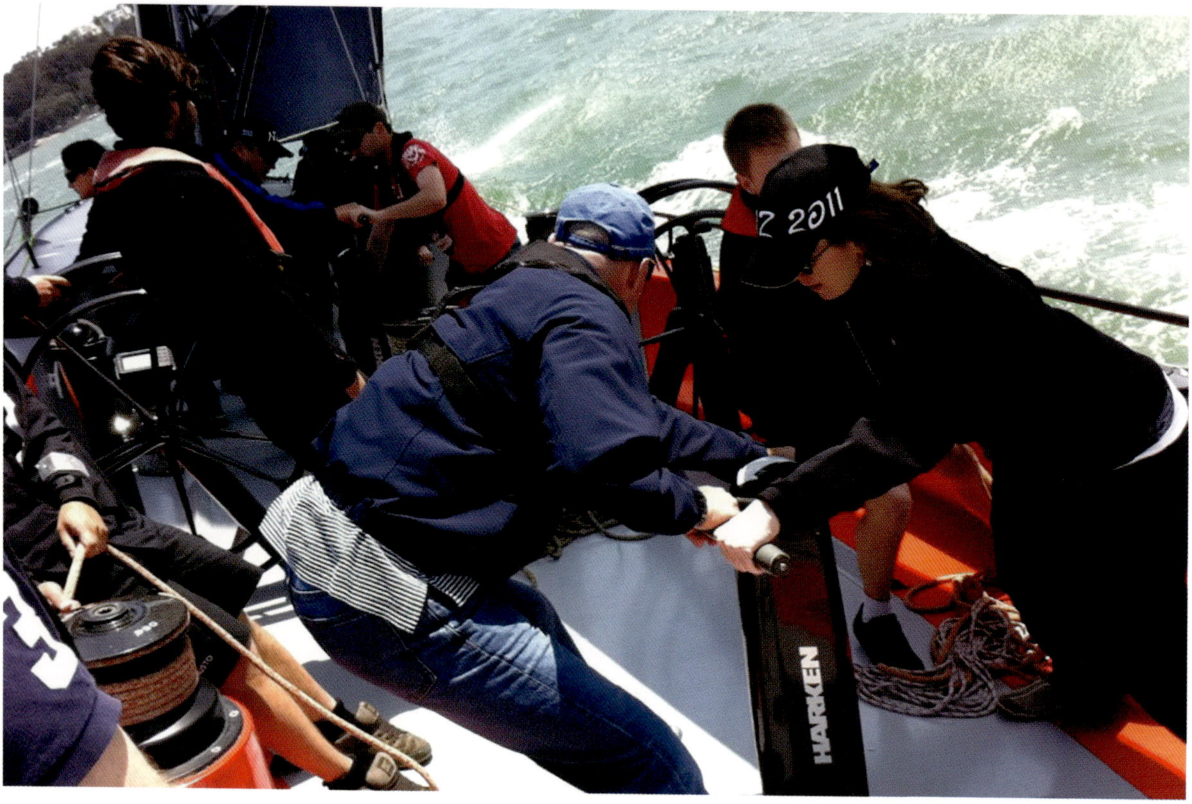

Z 2011
HARKEN

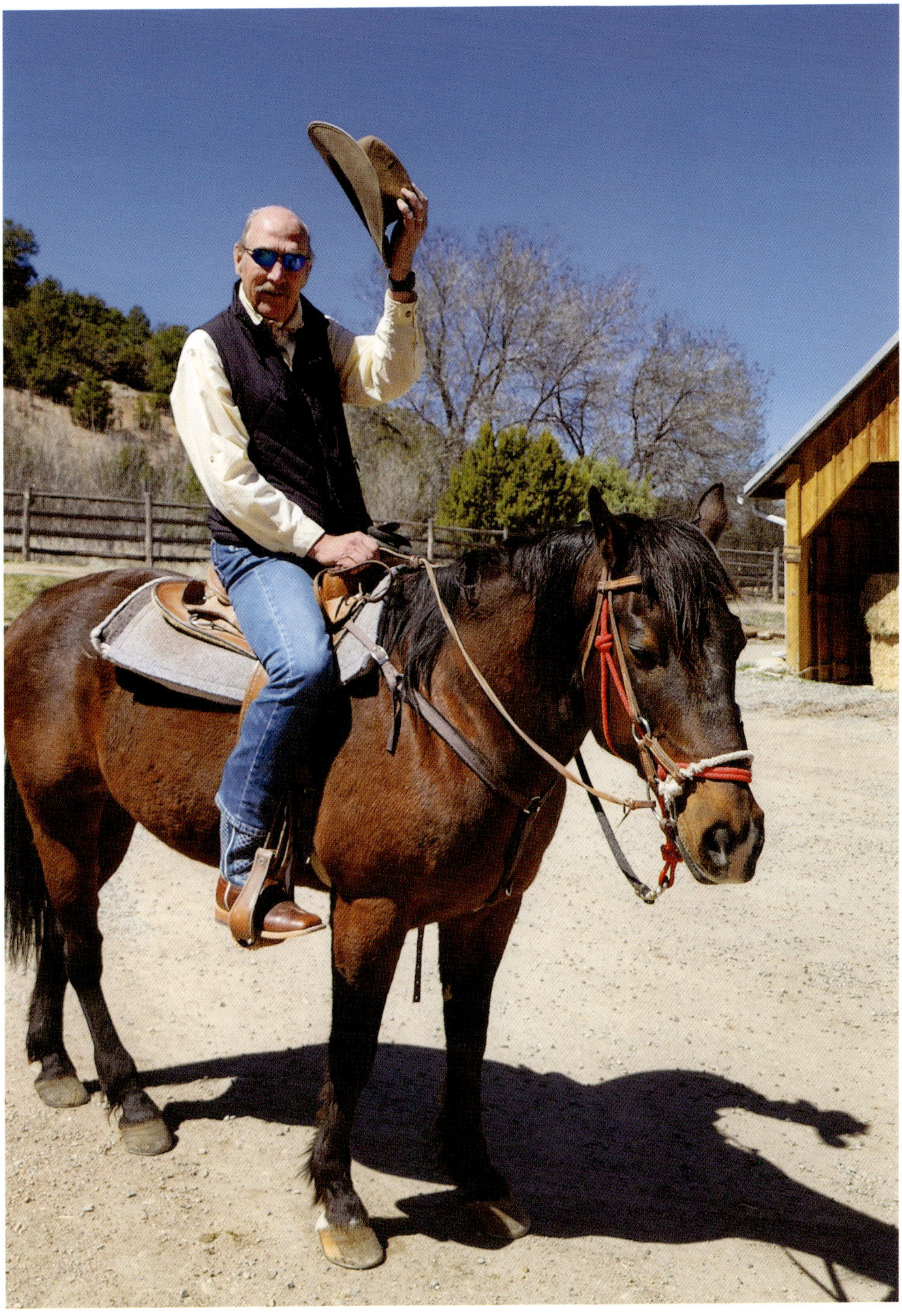

RECREATE

"I love to apply SERVE to family relationships. Creating meaningful moments around adventure and recreation is a powerful way to build bonds between parents and children, between spouses, and in your highly valued friendships. When you do something like go over a massive waterfall together or conquer a challenging hike—it builds those bonds in a dynamic way." —GARY NIEBUR

"In recent years, it seems that recreating, or 'playing together' as an extension of business relationships, has become less of a focus for some. The irony, of course, is that successful business is primarily founded on the strength of the interpersonal relationships which underpin any given transaction. To that end, we should be focusing more on the value of recreating, which fosters camaraderie while also recognizing shared competitive spirit and affording the opportunity to have a little fun. Mini tournaments, fun award ceremonies, and team challenges as a part of business events are lighthearted ways to effectively fuel stronger bonds between individuals or functions, without seeming like a deliberate or manufactured reason to do so."

—JONATHAN CLARKSON, CHIEF PRODUCT OFFICER AND VICE PRESIDENT, AIRLINE INDUSTRY

A level playing field also helps bond a group because it's horizontally balanced, so you end with high spirits where everyone can feel they were included or part of the win.

> "There's a vulnerability aspect with games. You know everyone's at different levels. You're not in your business gear. Your armor is off. But once you get going, you have a lot of fun. And there's a team aspect, too, so it takes the relationship to a higher level where it's not transactional. Human beings are social animals. You start to play, and you end up sharing things, you find out what you have in common, you have a connection now that you didn't have before." —KEVIN WARREN

"I had never swung a tennis racket before, but I got on the court with Stan and Gary. All of us did. And what I love is that they get you doing something you normally wouldn't. We organize into teams, try something new, get coached by you guys. This creates a great memory to share with our guests—something they'll go home remembering."

—DANIELLE VINCENT

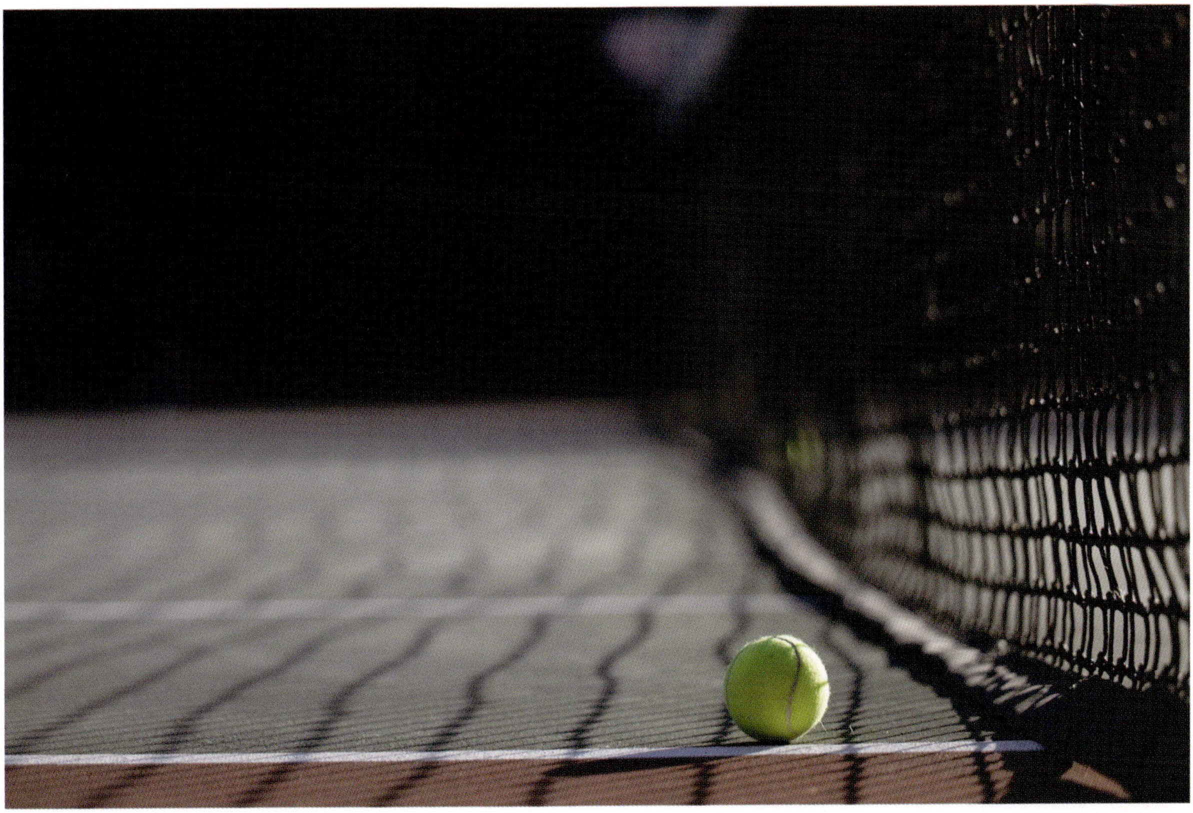

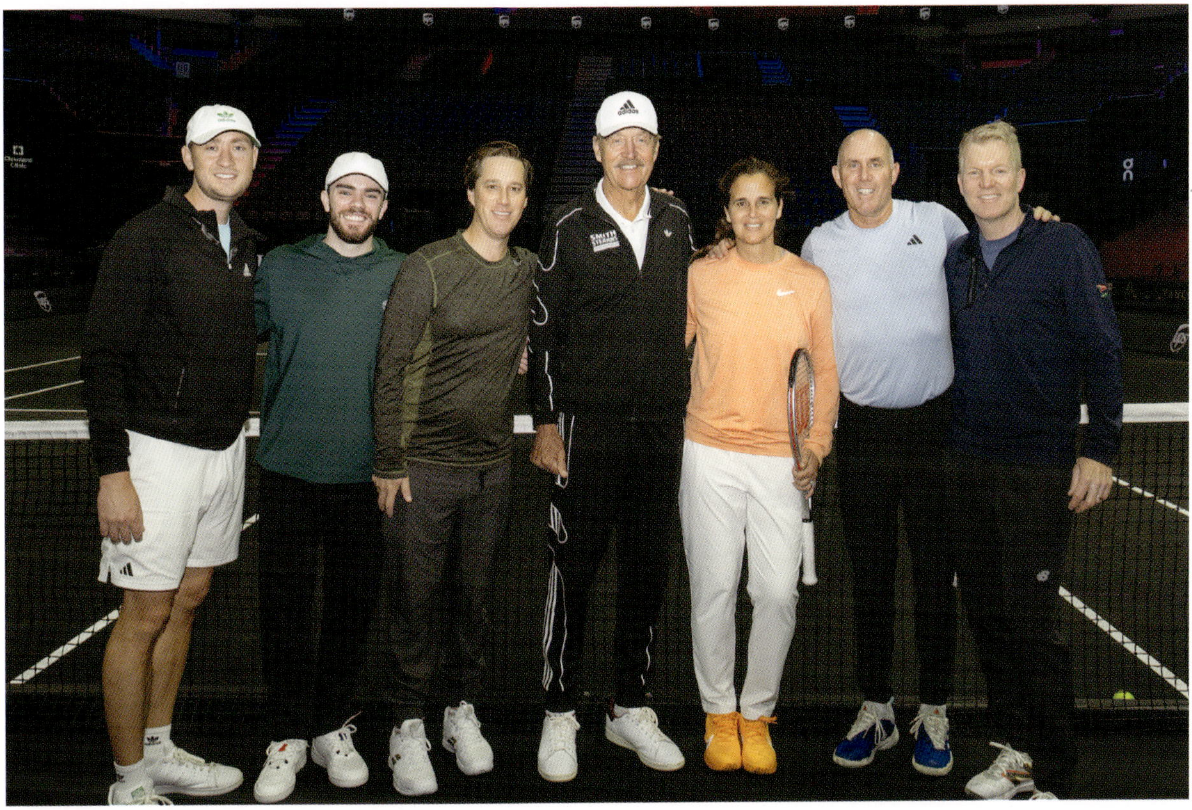

#2 PUSH THROUGH RESISTANCE

Right before games or play begins, we usually get some hesitancy. "Gary, I'm not like you…. I'm terrible at games!" "I've never thrown a horseshoe in my life." "I'll make a fool of myself in front of my coworkers." Expect some resistance. And do everything you can to coax people into the moment. Keep yourself in the moment. Joke around. Lighten spirits. The hardest part of playing is before you start. But then once you do—and if you let yourself be engaged in whatever ridiculousness, competitiveness, or beginner's luck ensues—you'll experience the connectivity and shared memory forming.

We've been running events for thirty years, and probably our heart rates are at their highest when we're engaging with our clients in play. We're hitting or tossing balls, cheerleading, lightly trash-talking, encouraging, throw-down challenging… all of it. We're at our peak levels of engagement. And it's incredibly rewarding. We watch people go from anxious and wary of playing, to laughing at themselves and cheering their teammates on as if it's the biggest business deal of their lives… and then to telling us afterwards it was a highlight of the whole thing.

Push through resistance and push others through pregame nerves. Don't give in to the temptation to cancel it and replace it with a meeting. Step up to the plate. Pick up a horseshoe. Huddle up with your team.

"I was at a Stan Smith Event in D.C., and out of the corner of my eye I saw Gary and his wife, Teresa, pedal away on bikes. In the middle of running an event, Gary made the space to recreate with his wife, and that's how you can see they practice what they preach. They really do play and believe it matters in their relationships. It's a very freeing, inspiring thing to watch and imitate." —ANN MASHBURN

#3 MARK THE MOMENT

Capping off recreation by gathering everyone back together to articulate and highlight all that happened helps mark the meaningful moment. It brings everyone back into a huddle, giving people the time to connect over the memories that were just created. And for whoever is leading or standing in front, it's an opportunity to call out the value of what you've experienced together. It's also a chance to engage once more by redirecting the spotlight onto others, call people out for their gifts and/or surprising talents, joke around, self-deprecate, and delight everyone with prizes and mementos.

When people share a moment that matters, a personal memento is truly meaningful to mark the moment. A physical item helps cement what happened in people's memories, so we love taking the opportunity to give each person something like a team photograph with the backdrop of the course they just played. We have clients and guests who keep these mementos displayed on their mantels, their desks, or their office walls. It's a way to extend the experience long after it ends. And it's one of those micromoments layered into the overarching experience that once again builds toward a significant moment that matters.

We had one of our clients and her guests for an unforgettable, multi-day event. Danielle Vincent, Fortune 500 Senior VP Head of Retail Card Services, is one of those all-around SERVE models in how she leads her team with intentional strategy sessions—engaging the whole person, recreating to create memories, volleying back and forth to solve problems, and elevating the details in a way that shows intentional and thorough care for the people she leads.

Danielle knows the value of giving her guests an unforgettable experience. Together, we created an event that mixed idyllic, challenging, and thrilling moments with family-style dining, fireside talks, glow-in-the-dark golf, and a closing ceremony where Stan and Danielle brought everyone together and delivered all sorts of mementos and gifts—from baby Stan Smith shoes given to new grandparents to a special bottle of wine for an aspiring sommelier. In the midst of all the spotlighting and honoring, they also engaged in some lighthearted humor and shared laughs. They memorialized moments that bonded people to one another. And Stan described how the shared experiences stemmed directly from people caring about each other—investing in genuine relationships instead of transaction or protocol. He praised Danielle for her intentions to build trust and elevate these moments for her people.

Call out what matters. Articulate the "why" behind what you're doing. Honor people and show them you care. Gathering back together at the end of an event is the perfect chance to do these things—and it caps off whatever experience you've designed with a poignant bookend.

NZL 68
SAILNZ
The Ultimate Sailing Experience
www.sailnz.co.nz
MUSTO
TOYOTA
Fly Emirates
Estrella Damm
NEW ZEALAND

NZL
41
SAILNZ
The Ultimate Sailing Experience
www.explorenz.co.nz
MUSTO
NEW ZEALAND
Fly Emirates
NEW ZEALAND

RECREATE

GAMES DON'T HAVE TO BE ALL-DAY, OFF-SITE AFFAIRS. BRING A GAME ON-SITE OR INTO YOUR HOME THIS WEEK. WHETHER IT'S INSIDE OR IN THE PARKING LOT, JUST MAKE SPACE. AT FIRST IT MAY FEEL AWKWARD TO INVITE A TEAM MEMBER OR CLIENT UP TO THE POP-A-SHOT HOOP FOR A FIVE-MINUTE COMPETITION, OR TO INCLUDE A GAME IN A FAMILY GATHERING, BUT YOU'LL SEE HOW PLAYING TOGETHER AND HAVING FUN DOING IT CREATES SHARED MEMORIES AND ULTIMATELY HELPS BUILD TRUST.

SOME IDEAS:

CORNHOLE

BOARD GAMES

TABLE TENNIS

KUUB

BUCKET GOLF

PUTT-PUTT GOLF

BIKING

AXE-THROWING

HIKING

PICKLEBALL

CROQUET

BOCCE BALL

SAIL RACES

ANY TYPE OF TEAM CHALLENGE

R

"You can't be too critical to receive ideas." —STAN SMITH

VOLLEY:
RALLY YOUR WAY FORWARD

Problem-solve with direction and optimism—letting ideas flow without defensiveness or ego—so the end result both solidifies trust and innovates into new spaces.

WE ALL FACE PROBLEMS TO SOLVE. Every business, every leader, every day. For a lot of us, we're leading teams or designing products and services because we love the act of solving something that's complex or wrought with challenge. So the choice we have to make is *how* we'll solve problems. And if you get the *how* right, it shifts the entire atmosphere.

After the 1996 Olympics, we started partnering with Danny Meyer for hosting events around the US Open and his restaurants in New York City. He had already paved a golden road in the restaurant world, opening iconic restaurants and making a big mark in hospitality. His book, *Setting the Table*, is a New York Times bestseller, and it reframes the idea of what it means to take care of people—the people who work with you, the patrons you serve, the community that receives you. He also hires people with a high "hospitality quotient," which includes kindness and optimism. We've learned invaluable lessons from watching Danny and his team, and so much of what Danny embodies resonates with how our Stan Smith Events team creates moments that matter. But one of the truly special lessons has been observing Danny's optimistic approach to solving problems.

About fifteen years ago, we started playing tennis together—but not the yellow ball sort.

We were about to host ten couples for the US Open, and they were flying in from all over the place. They were ready to see some incredible tennis in the Arthur Ashe Stadium, and we couldn't wait to host them. But all of a sudden, the weather forecast threw a curveball: 100 percent chance of rain. This was before the stadium had a roof. There would be no tennis. And when your overnight program is built around those matches, that's a huge problem.

So we called Danny. Danny knows New York City like the back of his hand, and we needed some quick and creative solutions that would feel like a beautiful alternative to our incoming guests. First, we brought all the facts forward—the uniqueness of our guest list, the timing of arrivals and departures, the budget. Then, as we were tossing ideas back and forth with Danny, considering all sorts of options and making calls to see what last-minute access we could secure, Danny asked, "Do you realize what we're doing? We're playing tennis! Instead of a fuzzy yellow ball, we're just hitting ideas back and forth, volleying and finding our way into a realistic, creative solution."

Danny was not only speaking our language, he was right. Our energy was high, we were optimistic and engaged, we were partnering with direction and ease. And in the end, we had a strategy that was fine-tuned and ready to deploy. We secured great tickets for our guests to a Broadway show—with backstage passes for a special tour and meet and greet. It was a hit.

Volleying ideas with Danny marked a moment that mattered for our team. It solidified the way we want to always approach problem-solving: **with optimism, self-control, and finishing well.**

WHO DO YOU ENJOY SOLVING PROBLEMS WITH?

WHO WOULD YOU SAY ENJOYS SOLVING PROBLEMS WITH YOU?

"I was twenty-seven and had just opened Union Square Cafe. I was complaining to my grandfather about how hard it was, and he said, 'It's time you learned the biggest part of business is problems. And your job isn't to try to eliminate problems—it's to solve them more creatively and generously than how others are doing it.'"
—DANNY MEYER

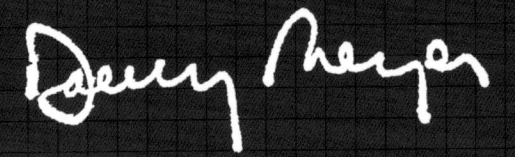

#1 BE OPTIMISTIC

Being optimistic is all about your energy and belief. You step into that room or phone call or session with the positive belief that you're going to figure things out—and you're there to be a willing participant in the process. You are realistic and bring all the facts forward, but with expectation. You put aside judgment, apathy, naysaying, and ego. Whatever problem you're facing, you are ready and enthusiastic to join your partner or partners in lobbing ideas back and forth until you find the one that nails it.

Volleying takes a high level of engagement. Just like we talked about in the Engage part of our SERVE framework, engaging others well means having humility and redirecting the spotlight. When you're problem-solving with optimism, humility looks like letting others have the floor to share their ideas. Volleying isn't a one-sided talent show. It's not a one-up game. Instead, you're optimistic that whoever is helping create the solution has value to add, even if they need some space to fumble forward and take a few second serves. Giving people that ease of space builds trust. Sharing ideas to solve a problem is often a vulnerable act, and as we know, this is the gateway to growing relationship and deeper trust. Vulnerable suggestions also open doors you haven't yet considered, and that's where innovation really takes off. And an optimistic, trusted partner makes vulnerability possible.

Michael Rittler and his successor, Danielle Vincent, have been two of our clients we love to volley with and design experiences alongside because even though they're incredibly clear on the "north star" of where they're headed, and they begin with the end in mind, they have both been completely open to doing things in fresh ways.

"We're trying to find that stickiness, that connectivity. Our clients have many choices of who to partner with, so I get to work with your team on thinking about every single moment and exceeding expectations—from the airport pickup to the atmosphere to the games. We toss ideas back and forth, and it doesn't get stale. We receive many thank you letters from our clients after the events, saying how it just keeps getting better and better, every experience they join. I think it's in part because we're willing to color outside the lines as we design these moments together."

—DANIELLE VINCENT

Even in a difficult or high-stakes situation, we believe optimism is critical to reaching a solution. It's tempting to shut down during the volleying process or shout from the umpire's box when a big problem drops. We got a taste of this at the FIFA World Cup in Rio.

> "We had just gotten into Rio to plan for our upcoming 2014 FIFA World Cup program, and we were scouting the site a few months before our clients and their guests would arrive. While we were driving through a tunnel, all of a sudden we couldn't move. The tunnel had been blocked on both sides, and a man was coming through swinging a bat. When he got up to our vehicle, he banged on Stan's side and kept walking.
>
> The Brazilian police force arrived and got everyone out of the tunnel safely, but what we quickly realized, after the adrenaline subsided, is that we couldn't bring our clients and their guests into a scenario like this. We needed an armed security detail and bulletproof vehicles. So we—along with our client—began putting a rapid plan in place before the guests stepped foot in Rio. It was intense problem-solving, and what made it work as well and quickly as it did is that we had trusted people with whom we could volley openly. We couldn't shut down or get divisive; we had to lean in and engage—with energy and honesty—as a unified team. We put all the facts on the table. And we modified our original plan with added security and armored vehicles."—Gary Niebur

Dramatic problems like a tunnel attack may not (hopefully will not) be frequent, but if you're out there creating valuable moments for others, something will likely happen that could disrupt the experience.

One of our clients, Ralph Andretta, faced an entirely different high-stakes problem, but his was in the financial world. Someone on his team accidentally transferred a substantial amount of money to the wrong bank account. Chaos and blame could have easily been unleashed and made the problem increasingly difficult to solve, but Ralph chose "up and out." He pulled a core team together, made up of people he knew would collaborate instead of deflate, and they devised a fix-it spree. He said it took three exhausting days, but they recovered the money. And they held together as a team.

Maybe you aren't naturally wired as an "optimistic" person, but if you reframe optimism as a tool for powerful problem-solving and trust-building, you will likely find that optimism suits all of us. It welcomes vulnerability. It increases innovation. And it stirs up enthusiasm for the next round of volleying.

> "How do you dig your way out of a problem? Stop digging." —RALPH ANDRETTA

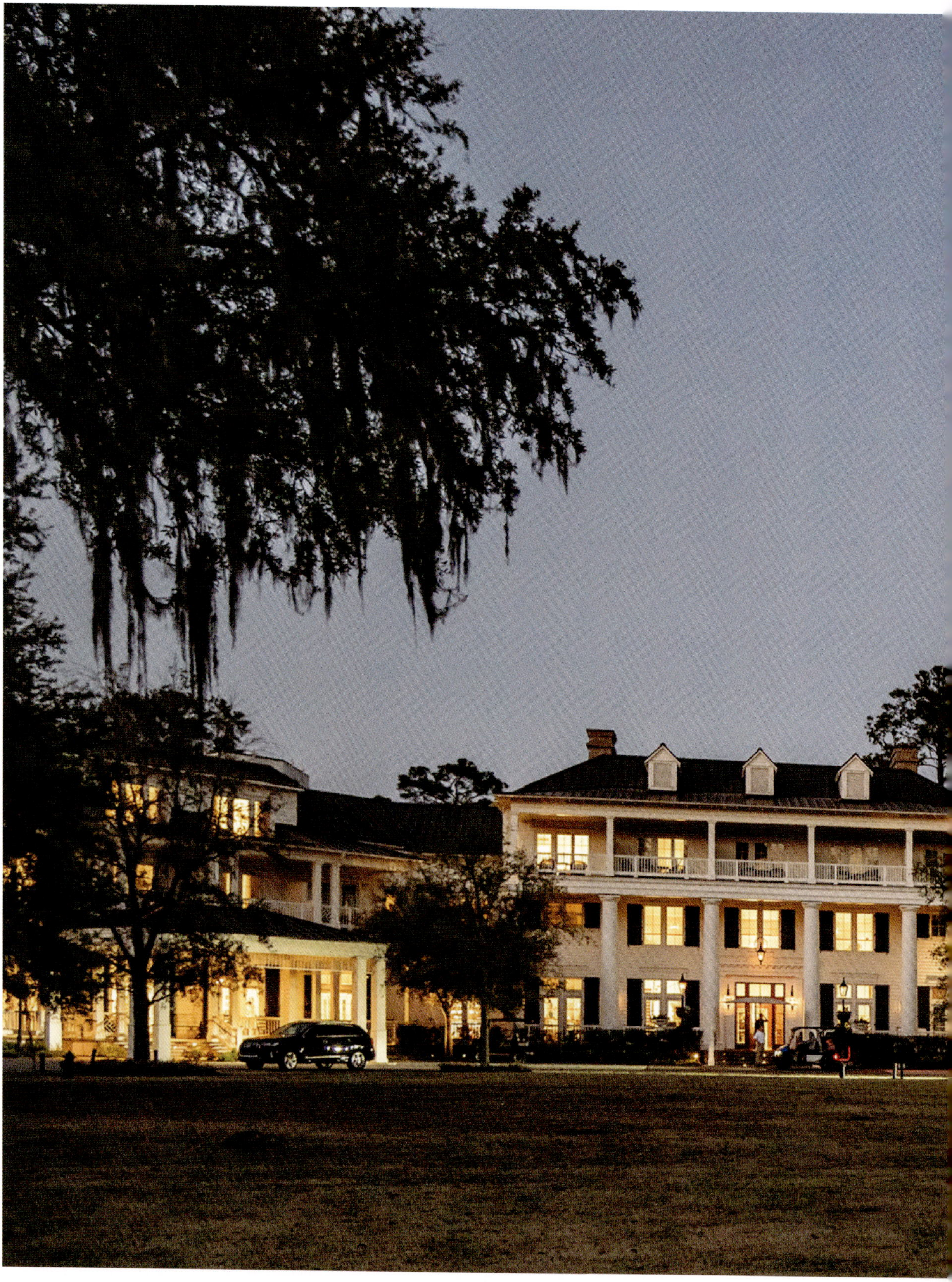

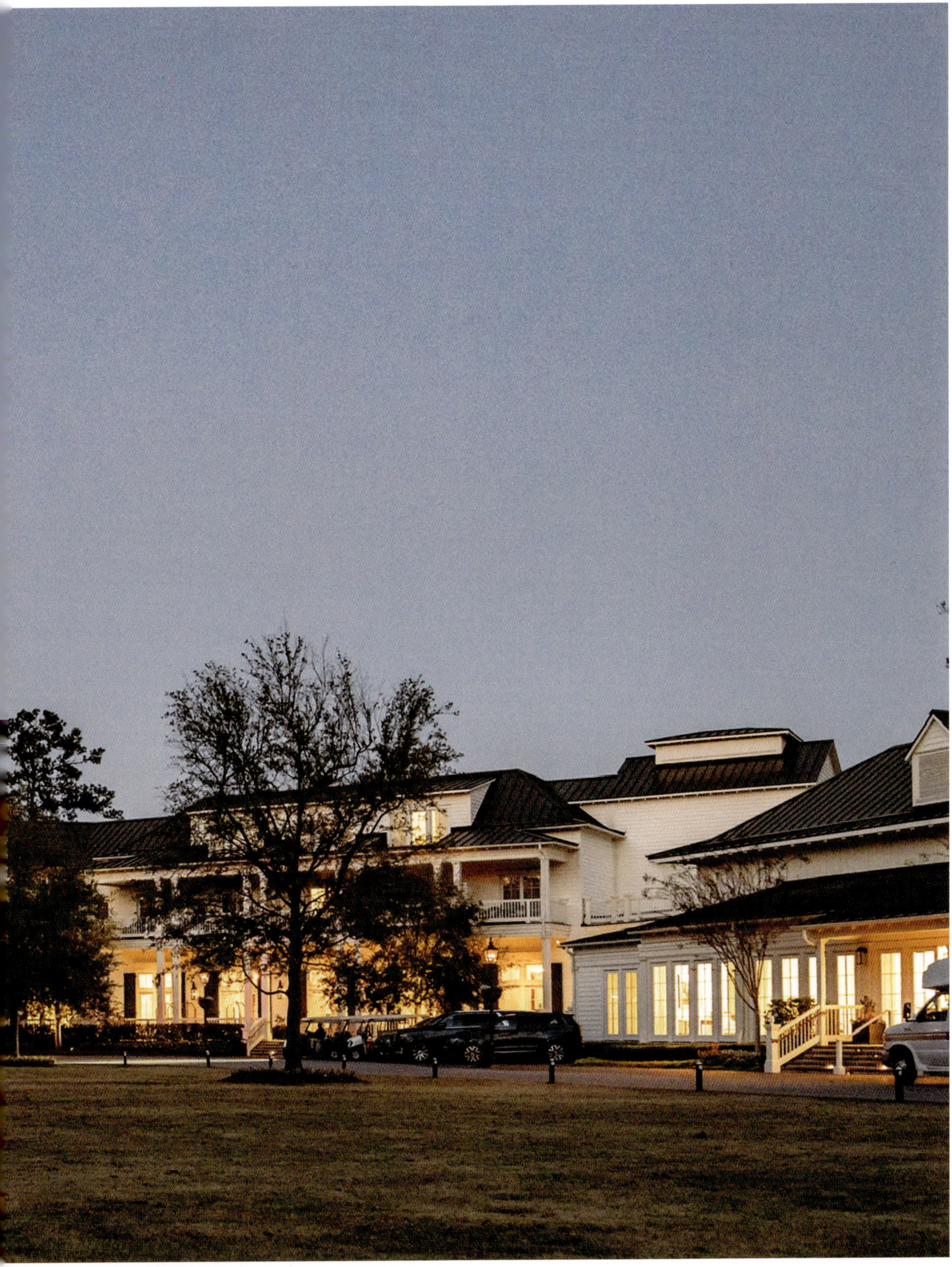

#2 HAVE SELF-CONTROL

Not surprisingly, the volley will be killed as soon as someone starts slamming.

If we ask someone to volley ideas around, then walk out onto the court and immediately start slinging power hits, our partner or teammates will either attempt to match our independent energy or turn down our offer the next time we ask to hit around.

There's nothing engaging about slams and power hits. Volleying is about continually building trust; it's trust in action. And we need self-control to reign in criticism, negativity, and blame (and encourage those we lead or work with to do the same) if we're going to accelerate trust in our valued relationships.

"Be open to receive ideas and not be too critical." —STAN SMITH

We heard this advice offered as a guide for solving problems in a marriage, but we think it applies just as well to any problem we're trying to solve, resolve, and move forward. It's called HALT. If someone is Hungry, Angry, Lonely, or Tired… postpone the volley. Sometimes these circumstances are unavoidable, but do what you can to set yourself up for success. Start when you're fresh in the morning, open the time with some engaging questions or compliments or banter. Frame the time by saying what you're hoping for: to simply generate ideas back and forth. Then listen really well, putting that self-control into practice. Don't interrupt or make judgmental faces when someone is sharing.

VOLLEY

VOLLEY

"I'm a visionary and get passionate about thinking outside the box, so I love volleying. I'm also working on being quick to listen and slow to speak, so that my team feels valued and becomes highly engaged in volleying too." —GARY NIEBUR

Try the "yes…and" where you build instead of tear down. Give grace. Some ideas people volley may seem terrible, but their next idea may be gold. Don't slam things and break the net.

When a team trusts one another, people on the outside will sense it. It's much easier to trust a team that trusts itself. When our clients and guests see us leaning into one another with confidence in real time, it gives *them* a sense of confidence too. Even when we're furiously paddling under the surface of the water, we keep calm and poised above water. This of course benefits the client, but it also keeps the energy balanced on our team. If someone is floundering, someone else needs to step in and redirect so that teammate has a chance to take a deep breath.

"Put each person in a winning position," is what Chef Michael Anthony says. "We're only as good as our newest team member, and if we're not helping lift them up, the guest experience will be less memorable, less wonderful."

CONSIDER ONE PERSON ON YOUR TEAM WHO YOU NEED TO PUT IN A MORE WINNING POSITION.
WHAT'S ONE SIMPLE WAY YOU COULD BRING THIS TO FRUITION THIS WEEK?
WHAT'S ONE MORE SIGNIFICANT WAY YOU COULD MOVE THE NEEDLE THIS YEAR?

VOLLEY

CONSIDER WHAT HABITS OR INSTINCTUAL RESPONSES YOU HAVE THAT COULD SHUT DOWN THE SPIRIT OF VOLLEYING. WHAT ARE A FEW CHARACTERISTICS THAT WOULD ELEVATE THE WAY YOU VOLLEY? START PRACTICING THOSE.

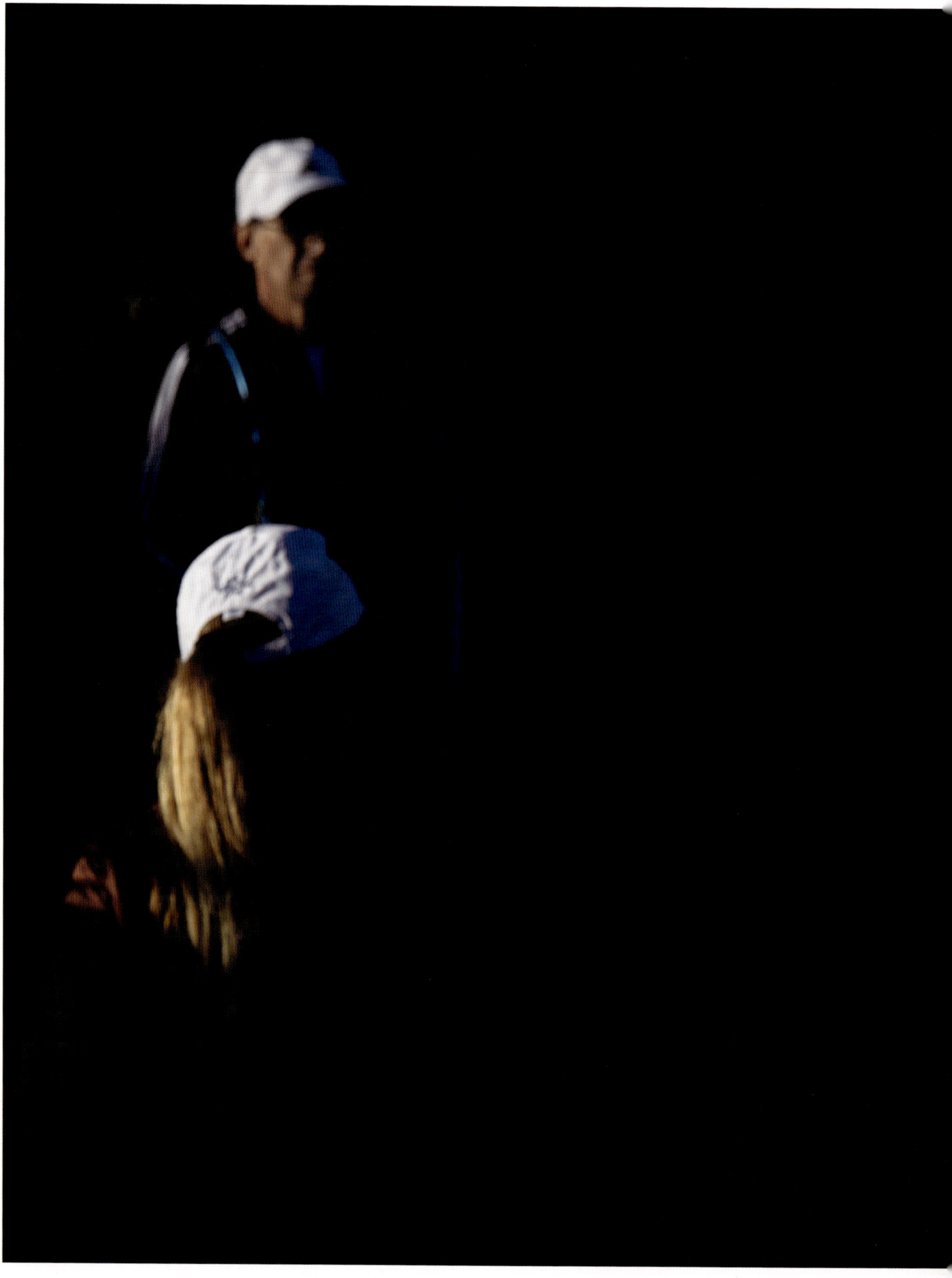

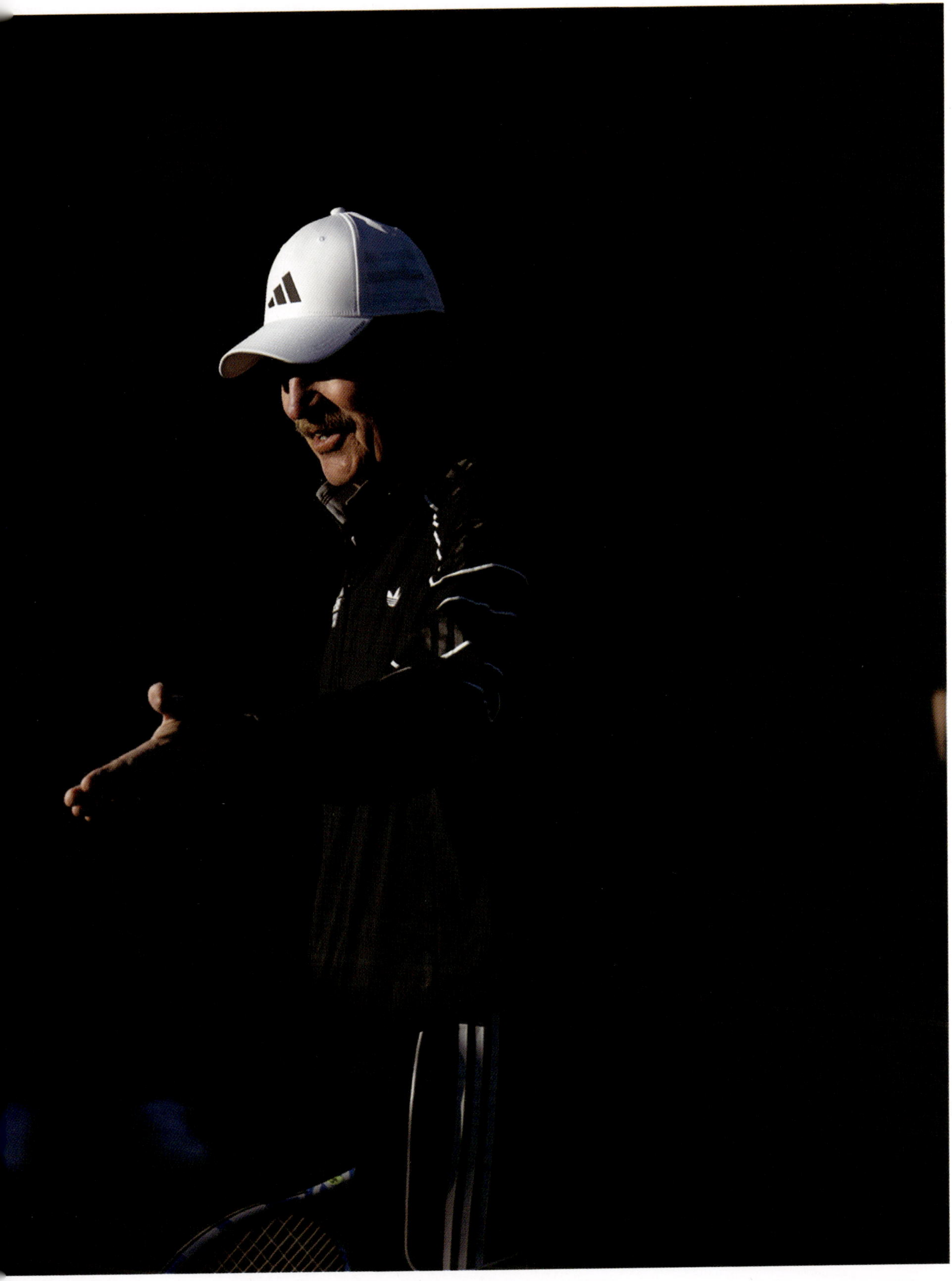

#3 FINISH WELL

Volleying doesn't end when the event—or the moment that matters—begins. Even if you've strategized a brilliant plan, figured out how you'll engage everyone involved, and identified a way to bring recreation into the right moments, you'll likely bump into a few walls right in the middle of your event. It'll storm when you're supposed to be outside, a significant flight will get delayed, a contract will have an error even though you've checked it fifty times.

As you mature in whatever role you're in, you get better at predicting what could go wrong. You learn to volley ahead of time to offset in-the-moment dilemmas. But when you step into a problem you didn't anticipate, you'll find your way out if you quickly admit it, own what's yours to own, and finish well.

Let's go back to Davis Love III's experience as captain of the US Ryder Cup. When his team lost in 2012, he went straight into conversation about how to help fix it for the next tournament—without having any idea that they'd give him a second chance as captain in 2016. He admitted where he and others fell short in the process, he invited honest feedback, and he didn't bow out. He problem-solved with the team because it was bigger than him: he wanted a win for the US. He finished well. And by finishing that job well, they chose him to lead them once again.

What we've seen proven again and again is that when you're on a team, it's much better to bring the problem to light immediately so everyone can rally and solve it together. This requires getting over our pride, because it's human nature to want to fix mistakes before anyone notices. But when trust is critical because you're trying to execute a complicated sequence of events, individual egos need to move to the back seat. An elevated and meaningful experience happens when everyone is transparent—and that means transparency needs to be rewarded by the rest of the team.

Another aspect to finishing well is simply landing the plane—finishing the volley session and activating the solution.

VOLLEY

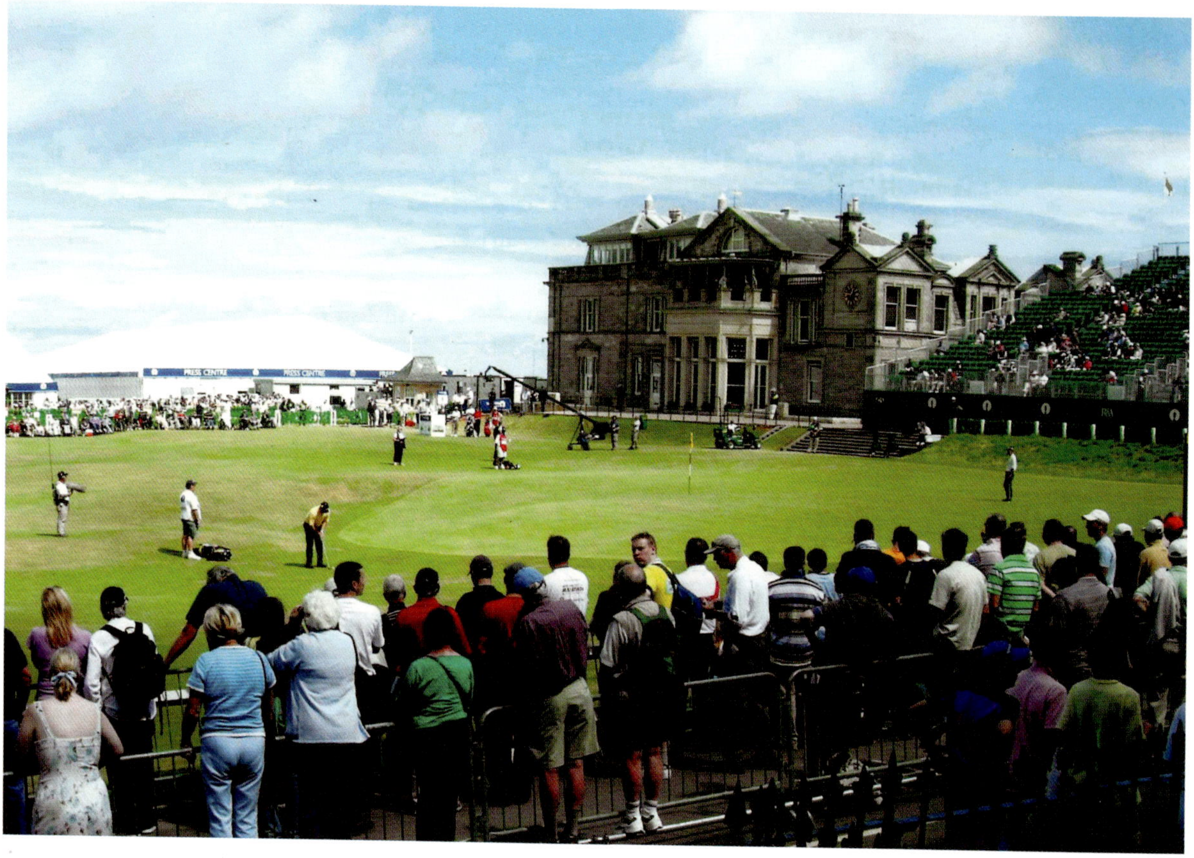

"We eliminated the silos in our organization. When I stepped into leadership, I saw there was a lack of cross relationships, and we needed to fix that. You can't be a team in name only; you've got to actually be a collective team who's meeting together, processing, debating, then solving to move forward. Once you determine the solution, the volleying is finished until you get a new round of facts. You don't stay on the court debating after you've decided the solution, and you don't splinter off into smaller teams and debate what the team decided. You volley to your solution and then stick with it." —STEVE SQUERI

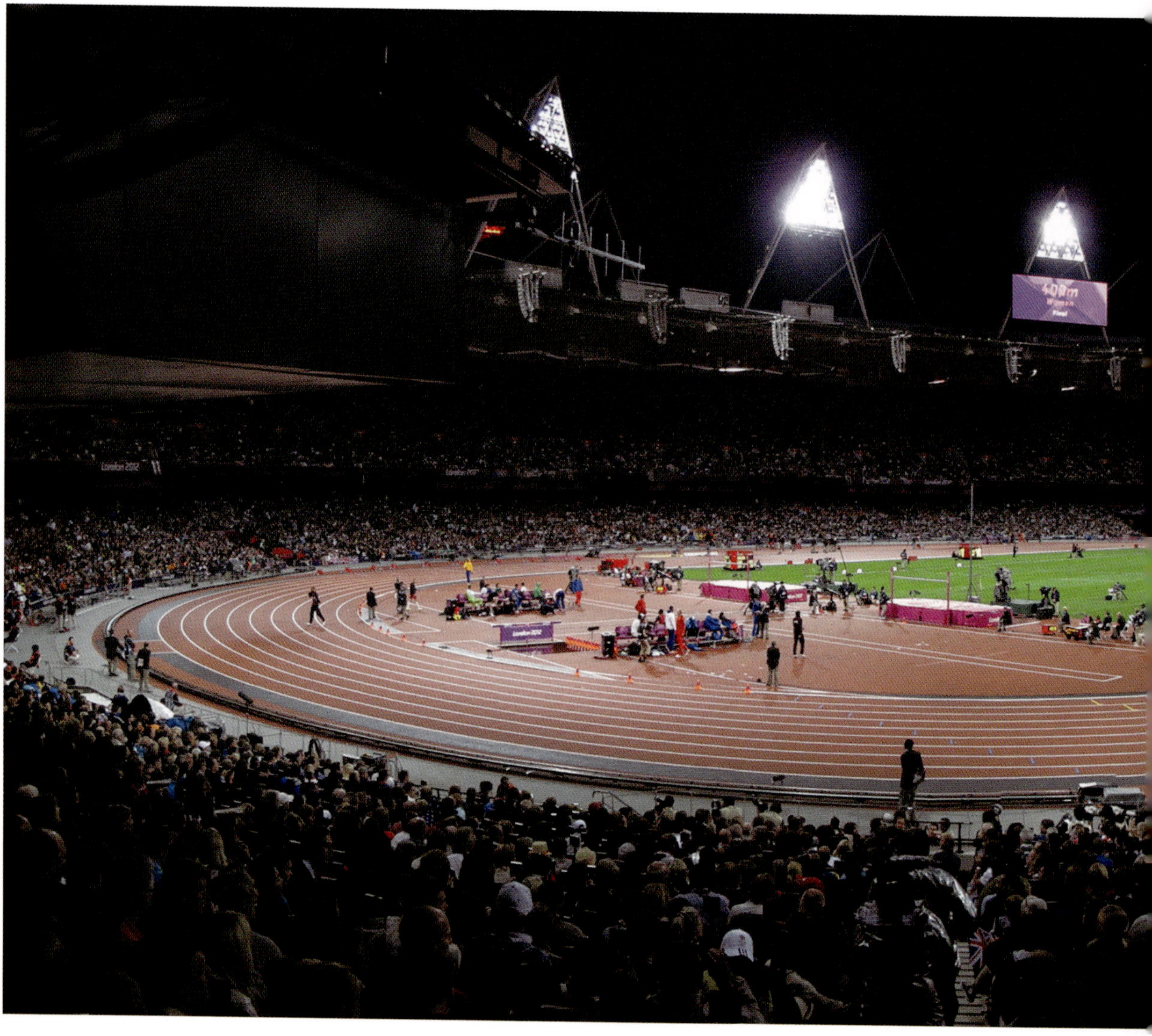
400m
London 2012

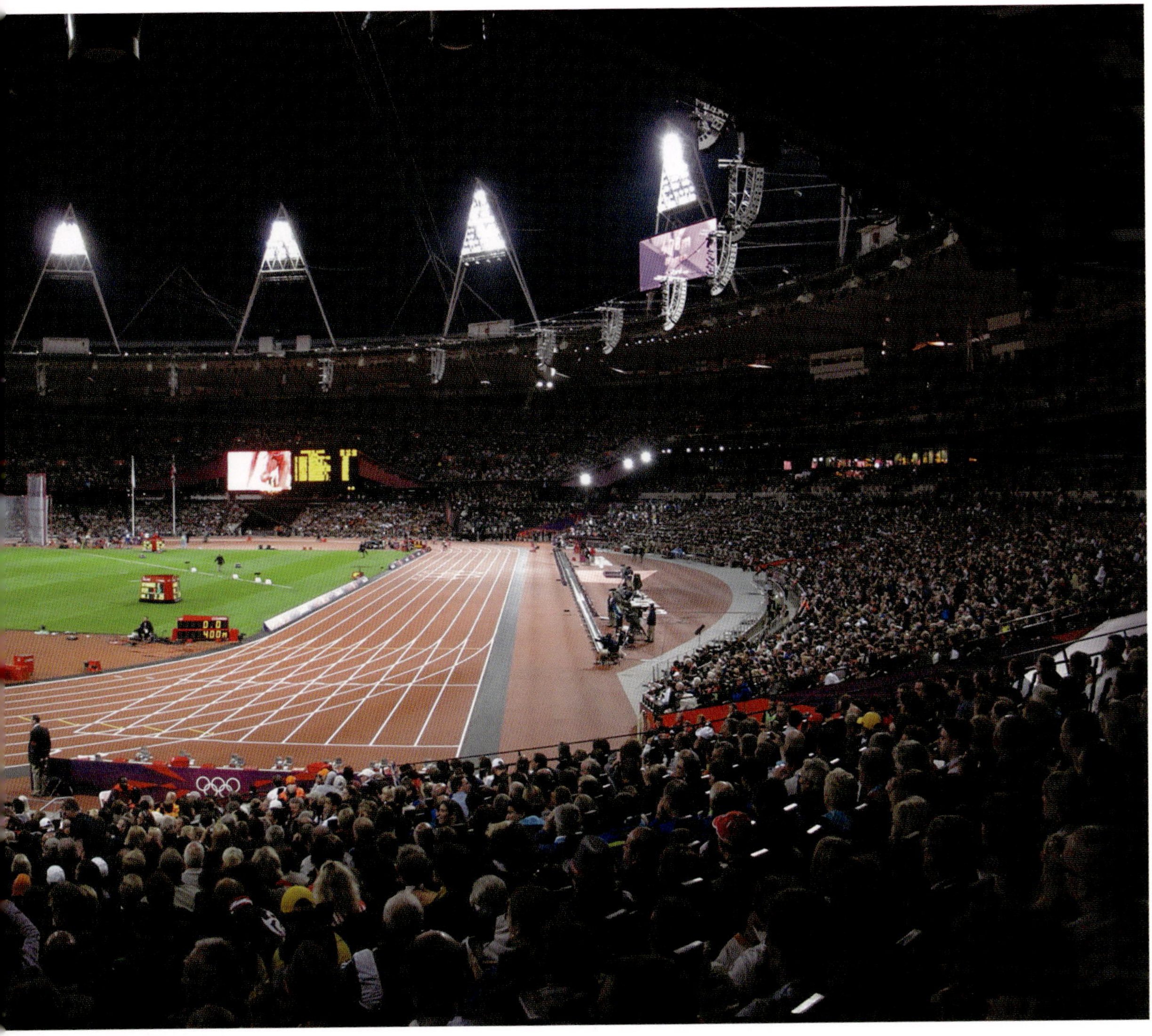

Sometimes in team meetings we realize we're spinning, stuck in the same place, instead of volleying our solution forward. It can happen if we don't have the right person in the room who has the best data or the ability to make the call, if we have too many cooks in the kitchen, or if we've begun to disengage and need to regroup when we can tackle problems with optimism and self-control. We've been learning to finish as well as we can, before we get stuck or disengaged, so that the next time we gather, we all trust the process once again.

When you hit walls in the middle of what you thought you already solved—those unforeseen backfires or roadblocks that crop up in the middle of a great plan—you still have the chance to finish well. You can reengage the volleying process and not only try to resolve it, but create a meaningful moment or connection between people because you gave it that extra, creative, and unanticipated attention.

We've also learned how to embrace impromptu, creative solutions from our partner, Lena Björck. Lena is a highly talented and resourceful caterer who has a knack for doing whatever it takes to deliver. We have many stories of Lena going above and beyond, which we'll get into in the next chapter when we talk about Elevate. But she's also a great example of finishing well.

Lena had been hired by a huge corporate client to cater a Saturday evening dinner in London. But Friday night, all her guests showed up to the door expecting a beautiful dinner. Clearly, they were a night early. At first, completely caught off-guard, Lena thought they were joking. But one look out the window at the well-dressed group waiting to be served told her otherwise. Instead of blaming her client for completely missing the mark and the contract they signed, she went into volleying mode with her small team. After handing out chilled drinks to the guests, her team started running around the streets of London grabbing whatever they needed with a clear vision in mind: solve it without letting the client know anything was amiss. Lena entered the back door into a fine-dining restaurant that had a private dining room still available, and she volleyed with their staff to create an impromptu meal with the ingredients they had on hand. She ran to a florist for fresh flower table arrangements while someone else bought vases. When her guests were seated in front of canapes and smoked salmon, filets and wines and bouquets of flowers, they never realized what Lena and her team pulled off behind the scenes, and what they never put back on their client's plate. With this competent volleying on her team, and willingness to own the problem without hesitation, Lena accelerated trust radically—and that client has recommended Lena again and again.

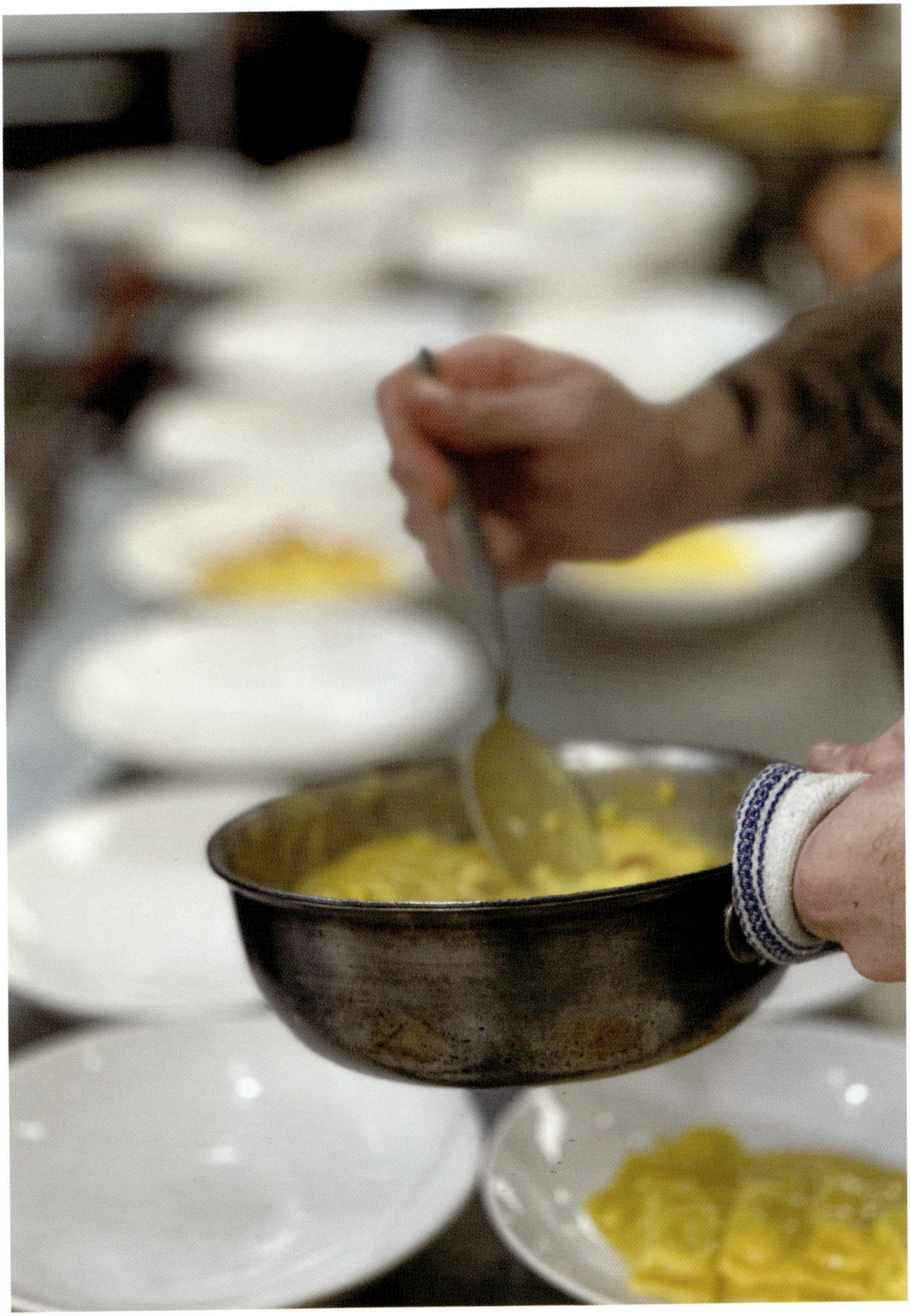

"If the captain is panicking, the players will panic." —DAVIS LOVE III

"When it rained at Roland-Garros, before they had a roof, we wondered where it would lead. Within minutes, Gary and Stan figured out a new way to make it a special experience. They got us into the Players' Lounge…you can't even buy a ticket to get in there. We ran into Rafa, and he was generous with his time, then turned around and there was John McEnroe. The rain, of course, didn't matter anymore."

—KEVIN WARREN

VOLLEY

"Try not to make your problems their problems."

—HAP KLOPP, FORTUNE 500 PRESIDENT AND FOUNDER

IS THERE ANYTHING YOU COULD PICK BACK UP AND FINISH WELL—WITH THE INTENTION OF BUILDING OR REKINDLING TRUST IN AN IMPORTANT RELATIONSHIP?
ARE THERE SOME SKILLS YOU MAY NEED TO DEVELOP TO GET BETTER AT PROBLEM-SOLVING?

HOW CAN YOU APPLY *SERVE* TO SOMEONE YOU NEED TO IMPROVE YOUR VOLLEY WITH?

"An amazing event can go sour if the bus isn't there on time." —STAN SMITH

ELEVATE:
CHASE DOWN EVERY BALL

Nail every detail so the entire experience exceeds expectations with special invitations, unique access, customized gifts, or surprise moments that solidify a trusted relationship.

NO MATTER HOW BEAUTIFUL THE STRATEGIC PLAN AND DESIGN OF AN EVENT, if the event itself isn't executed with precision, trust deteriorates and often breaks. Just like the discipline it takes to volley well, elevating the details also requires discipline—and will protect the newly-formed trust that flourished during a good volley. **If you don't hit all the small things, there won't be room for the big things to happen.** So you have to excel in the delivery—chasing down every ball as each moment unfolds—so that your clients, guests, and partners can relax into the experience you've designed and focus on what they're there for: each other. That's how you can deliver what they're expecting: a seamless, premier-level experience.

Hospitality is taking exquisite care of people. They may not see all the intricate ways you're taking care of them, but they will feel it. They will sense the security and ease, and this creates space for all the moments of surprise, delight, recreation, and connecting that are core to the experience.

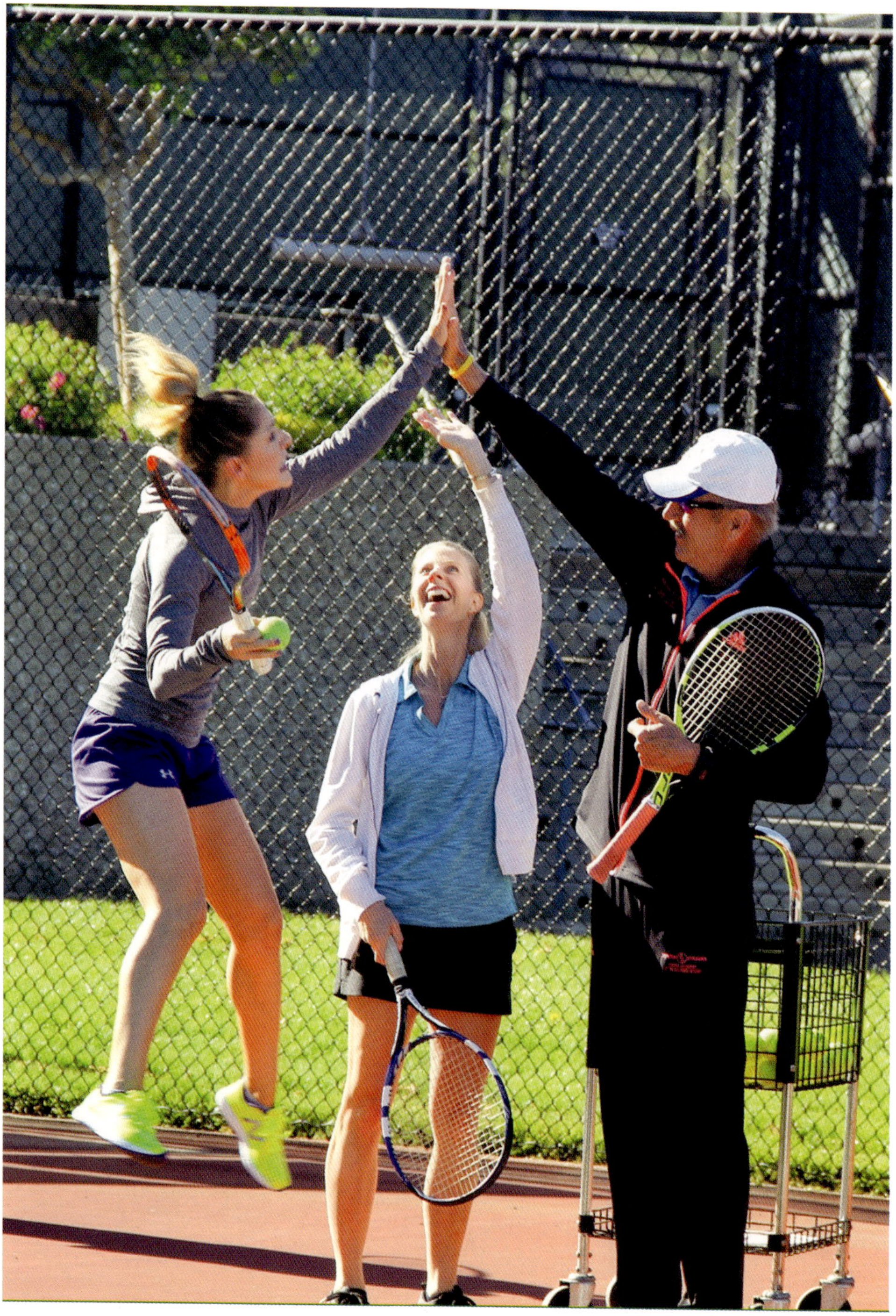

Deloitte.
CHUBB
CADILLAC
IHG
CHASE
ARTHUR ASHE STADIUM
us open
3 CARLOS ALCARAZ
22 FRANCES TIAFOE
J.P.Morgan
2022

"When I met Gary and Stan, I was a client of a client. We were at the Atlanta Olympics in '96, and as I observed and watched what they were creating for our group, I could tell quickly that we were cut from the same cloth. It's super complicated, what Stan Smith Events does—so many moving parts. The hard-to-get tickets. The hired talent that suits their guests. The unique places to eat. It's not just an 'add water' effort. It is detail after detail after detail that becomes an experience people walk away from and say, 'I couldn't have gotten that anywhere else.'"
—DANNY MEYER

ELEVATE

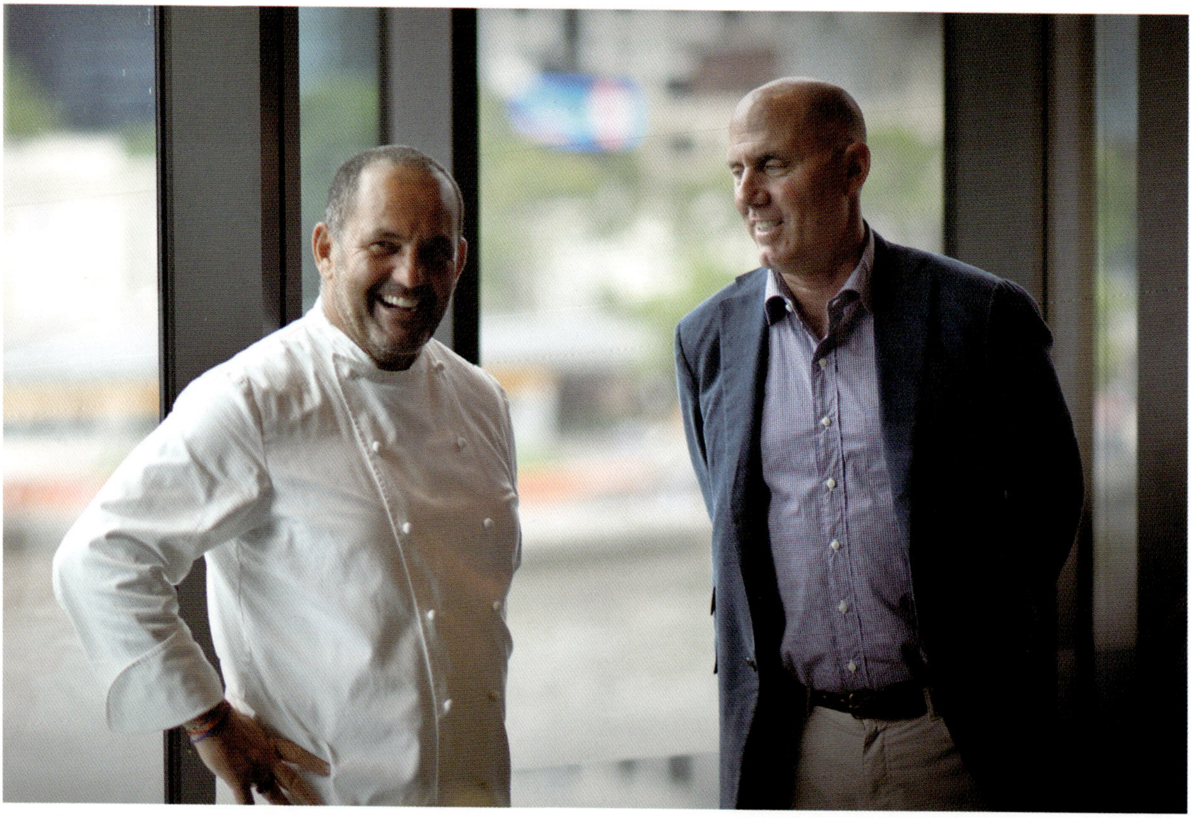

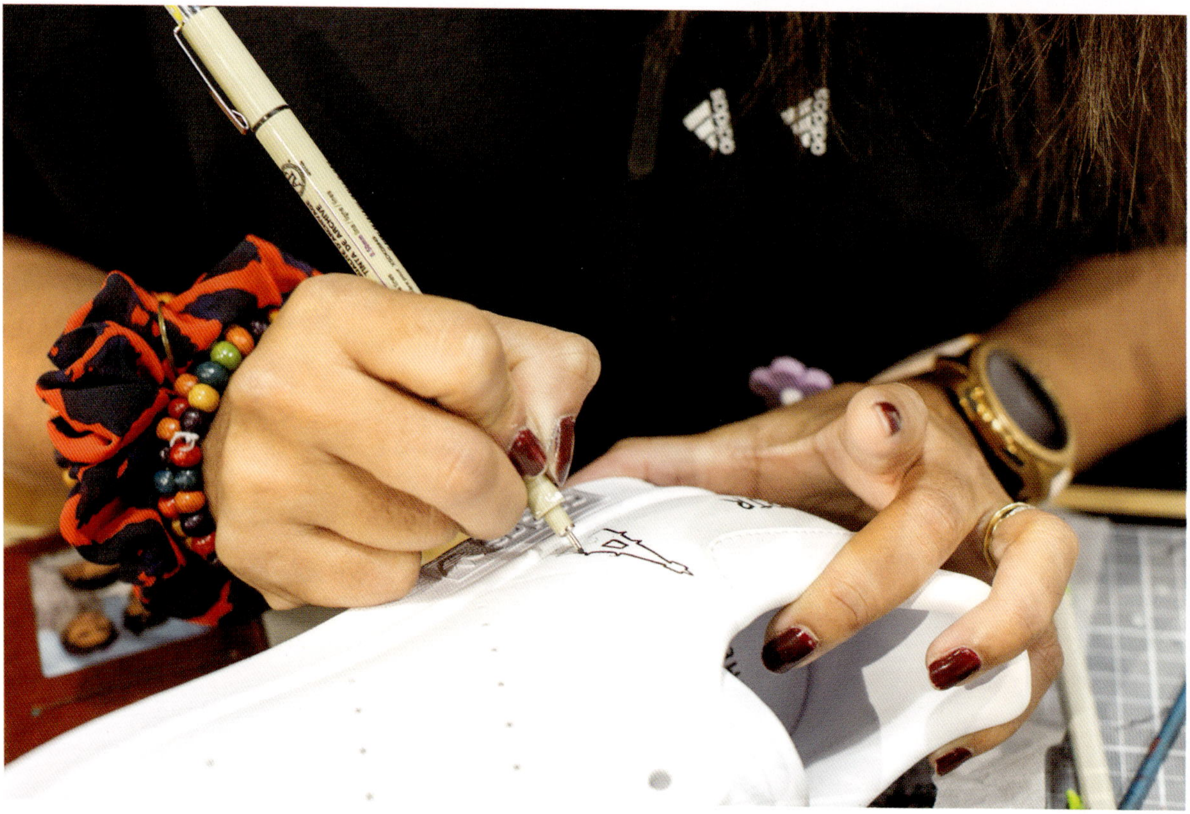

ELEVATE

Years ago, when we started doing events at Wimbledon, we hired Lena Björck, whom we shared about in the last chapter. Lena was new on the scene, but her engaging character and gumption felt promising. She more than delivered, and she modeled something we hold close: Lena is very good at elevating the details to deepen the bond of trust with her customers, partners, and clients.

> "The same night Lena won the prestigious Businesswoman of the Year award in London, she didn't miss a beat. With her award and bottle of champagne next to her, she jumped in her truck, drove all night, boarded a ferry, crossed the English Channel, and set up a meal for our clients at the House of Deutz in Champagne, France. It was incredible. Even after accepting a major award, she didn't let us down. She went above and beyond to get a beautiful meal planned, prepared, and delivered from one country to the next."—Gary Niebur

To chase down every ball and elevate an entire experience into one that really matters, you need a team where every member knows exactly what part they'll play. You need everyone to hold to the established standard. And you need to keep engaging during the experience itself (in all the micromoments of opportunity) by building on what you know about your guests' lives and deepening that relationship through paying attention.

CELEBRATING THE POWER OF TENNIS
2024
CELEBRATING THE POWER OF TENNIS

#1 PLAY YOUR PART

We're a lean team at Stan Smith Events. We keep it this way on purpose, because it fits with our family-style culture and helps us hold the boundaries we've set to limit the number of events we'll host. This gives us the space to elevate our experiences without cutting corners or wearing too many hats all at once.

When you're building up to a moment that matters, it's critical to get really clear on who does what. For our team, we know who's holding the reins on the itinerary, who's the boss of communications, who will deliver cold drinks to the vehicles, and who will get highly engaged with specific clients and not be distracted by logistics. Differentiating roles can sometimes feel tedious, but it's critical in a fast-paced and heavily facilitated experience. Because if we don't have our specific roles, we bump into each other. We create unnecessary chaos. Or we won't have our eyes on engaging with clients and guests in those pivotal, organic moments.

As a team, we do highly detailed run-throughs before every event (and then afterwards). We drill through all the minute-by-minute logistics to make sure we know who's doing what. We remind everyone of people's likes and dislikes, when we're dropping surprise gifts into hotel rooms, and which moments need to really shine. Even in run-throughs we'll sometimes find something we missed, or questions will come up because we've taken the time to review all the nitty-gritty. And it's the nitty-gritty that elevates our events in a memorable way and earns us repeat business because people trust our process.

"The reality of building trust with people is that 1) They need to know they're genuinely needed. This is essential within teams and also for the guests invited into these moments. And 2) You have to be relentless. The mental work, the preparation, the physical setup, the communication that exists before guests are anywhere in sight must be planned well and planned appropriately. We take ourselves out of our shoes and put ourselves in a guest's position. How do we meet expectations first, but then how will we exceed expectations in the moments themselves?"

—MICHAEL ANTHONY

"The team's organization is first-rate. You would never know as their client or guest if something had gone wrong. It's just executed that well. No one else we've worked with is as seamless and well-planned. The experience is incredible."

—TRACEY BOWRA

After the run-through as a team and making sure everyone knows the part they're playing, whoever is leading the event will get on location two or three days early. They meet with everyone who's playing a role in the event, from restaurant managers to pro shops and ticketing. The goal is ironclad execution. Inevitably, we have to volley again and put out small fires in these couple of days—perhaps our location for an open bar got booked by another group, and now we need to find a hospitality suite or alternate spot for our clients and guests to wind down in the evening. Or maybe an event earlier in the day got amended, so now we have to tweak the timing because it has a trickle-down effect on everything else on the itinerary. Maybe the guest list changed, so you re-strategize who's seated by whom, or if the panel discussion needs to adjust based on the new information.

Our early preparation is our chance to right the ship and get it back where it's supposed to be headed with our client's objective front and center. This is where there's a lot of payoff for thoroughly engaging with clients: they trust us to get behind the curtain. Then, in the moment, we're well informed and can help steer the event in the direction of our client's unique goals.

ARE THERE "RUN-THROUGHS" YOU'RE SKIPPING THAT WOULD ACTUALLY BE USEFUL—EVEN IF BRIEF?
PUT ONE ON THE CALENDAR.

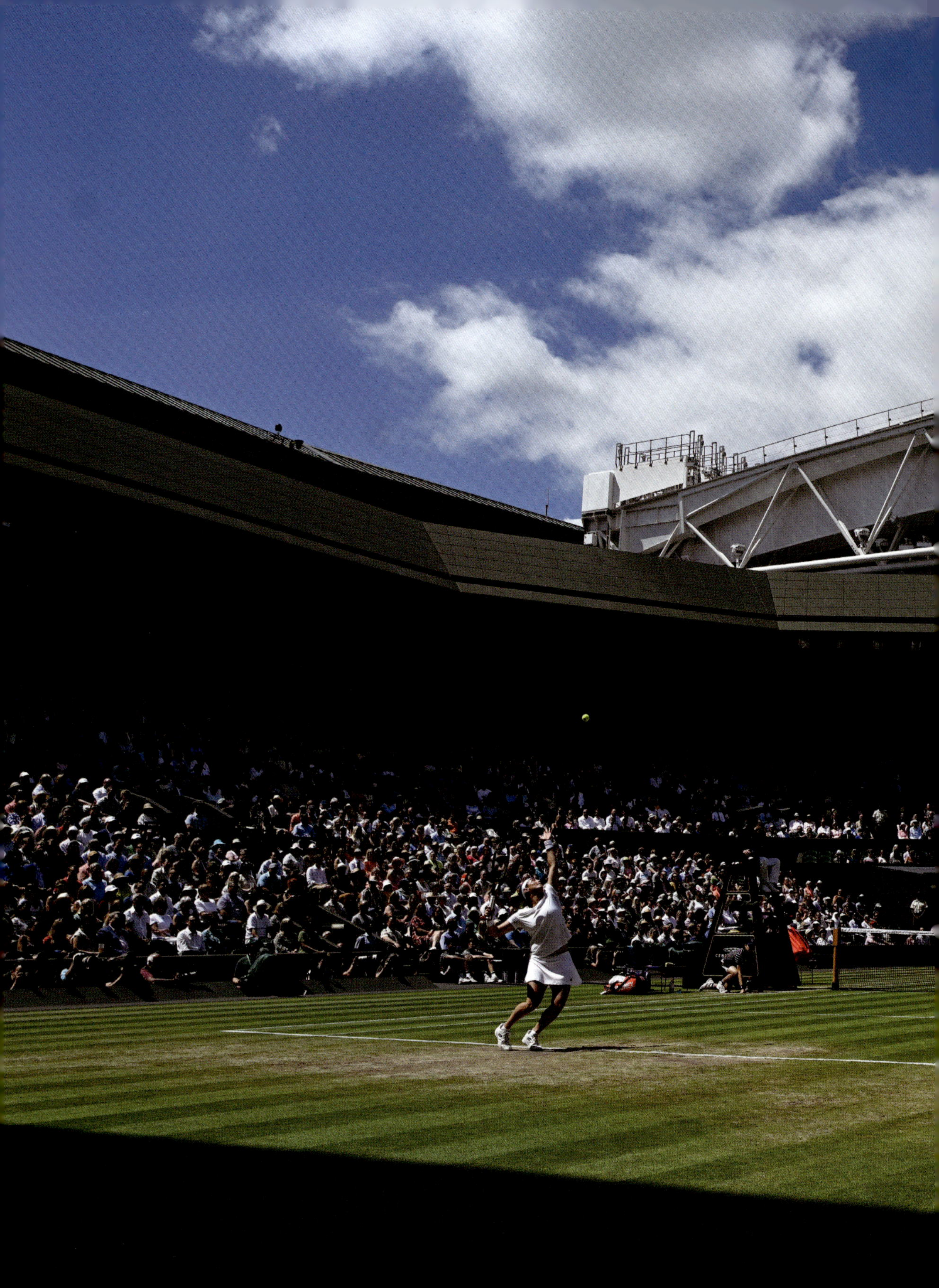

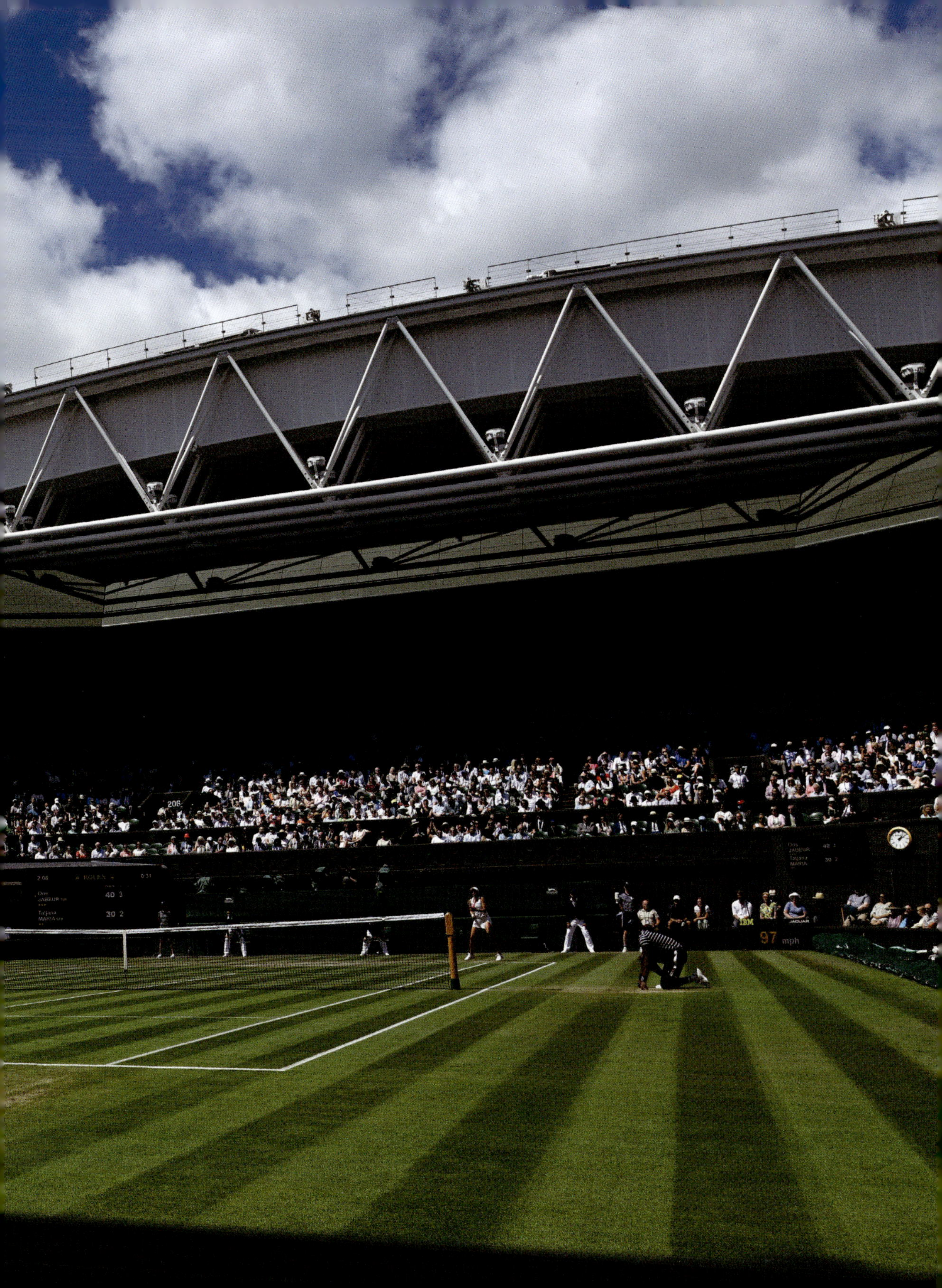
97 mph

#2 HOLD YOUR STANDARDS

Some years ago, we had a client who did an event at one of the Grand Slams, and we created a tennis clinic function for the guests alongside the tournament itself. Our client's event team wanted every guest to get a tennis racket. However, they didn't have the budget to get one worth its salt.

If you cut corners and lower your standard, people will feel it. If you skimp on the details and rush past all the little decisions, you will miss the great finale. It's like John Wooden, coaching legend, who started every season by teaching his team how to put on their socks and tie their shoes. Because there's a right way and a sloppy way, and if you're sloppy, you get blisters. If you're sloppy, you create fissures and shaky foundations. You have to nail the nitty-gritty, the fundamentals, the schedule.

Elevating an experience into a moment that matters means you hold to that high level. You know what you stand for, and you follow through.

"I brought the issue to Stan and Gary, and they wouldn't agree to skimp. They said, 'Absolutely not, we can't put our name behind it because it's not a quality product, and not synonymous with who we are.' So they leaned into their relationships to find a new solution, and get a better racket for their client's gifts. But they were to the point where they were willing to actually lose money on that budget line item to make sure the quality was upheld."

—CHRIS WHITE, STAN SMITH EVENTS TEAM

"Every piece of what we do points back to honoring relationships and creating a refined, boutique experience where you don't cut corners or sacrifice quality. I think this is what sets us apart."
—LINDSAY ERNST, STAN SMITH EVENTS TEAM

"You guys turn the memory around quickly. Even while we're still at the event, your team gets photos printed or awards framed before we leave, so we get to walk away with a memento. It brings a really warm memory...we hang onto all of it."
—RALPH ANDRETTA

WHERE DO YOU OR YOUR ORGANIZATION NEED TO PRACTICE "PUTTING ON YOUR SOCKS?"

DO YOU HAVE A MOMENT THAT MATTERS COMING UP? START PREPPING FOR IT.

#3 ACT ON WHAT YOU'VE LEARNED

When you're engaged in the moment, asking questions, modeling vulnerability, and helping people feel welcome and safe, they usually open up. You learn about their jobs, their lives, their children, the problems they're trying to solve—and you are in prime position to offer a real-time gift in the form of connection. It shifts a relationship from transactional to relational, and that's a critical shift when you're talking about trust.

Trust grows as people believe you're genuinely interested in their life—beyond the event or moment itself. If you've engaged well, these are the details that organically get shared while you're relaxing around the dinner table, playing cornhole after work, or sitting next to each other at a sporting event. So when you interact again, now you know what follow-up questions to ask. You have insight into what they care about and can surprise them with a memorable gift.

As a past Wimbledon Champion, Stan is invited to the Royal Box for the Men's Final. Over the years he has gotten to know William and Kate. When they had their third child, Louie, Stan had a pair of baby-sized Stan Smith Adidas shoes ready to give Kate in the Royal Box. Kate beamed at the thoughtful gift.

People love to be known. So whenever you can show people you're paying attention to what they've shared with you, it helps take your relationship to the next level.

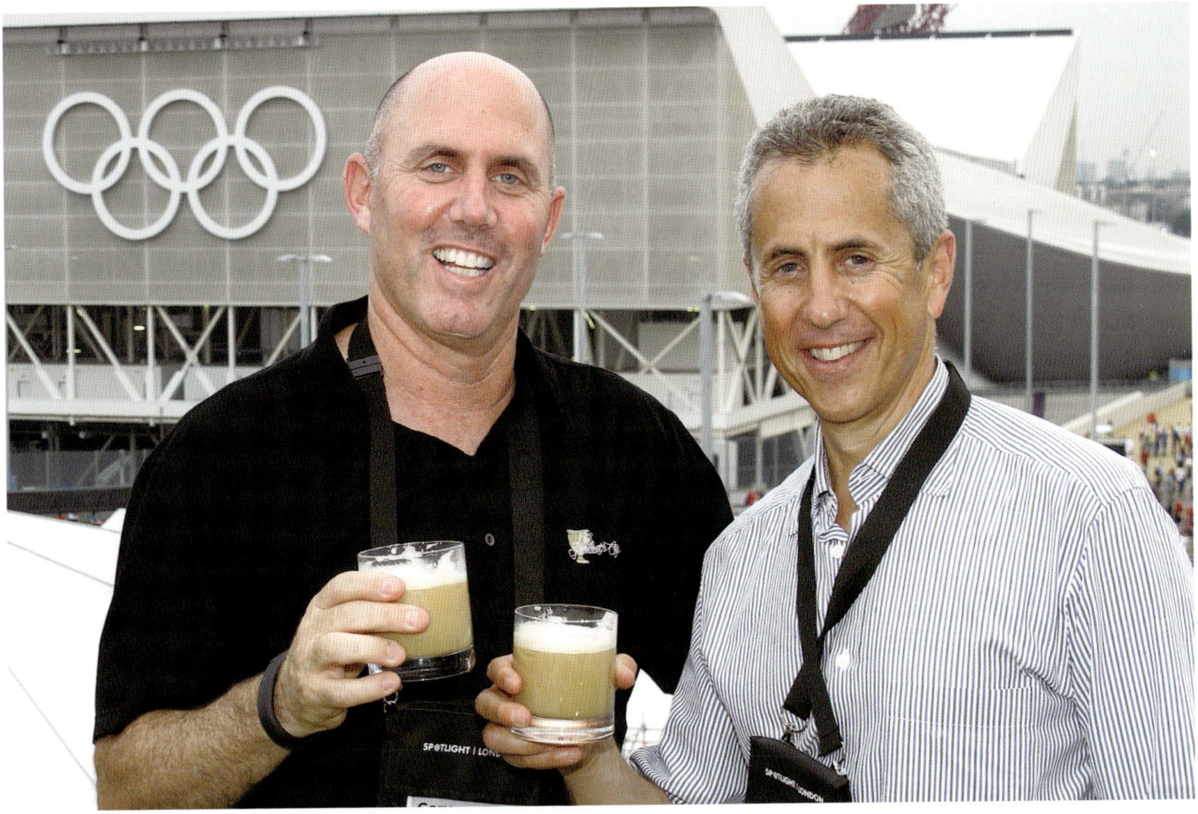

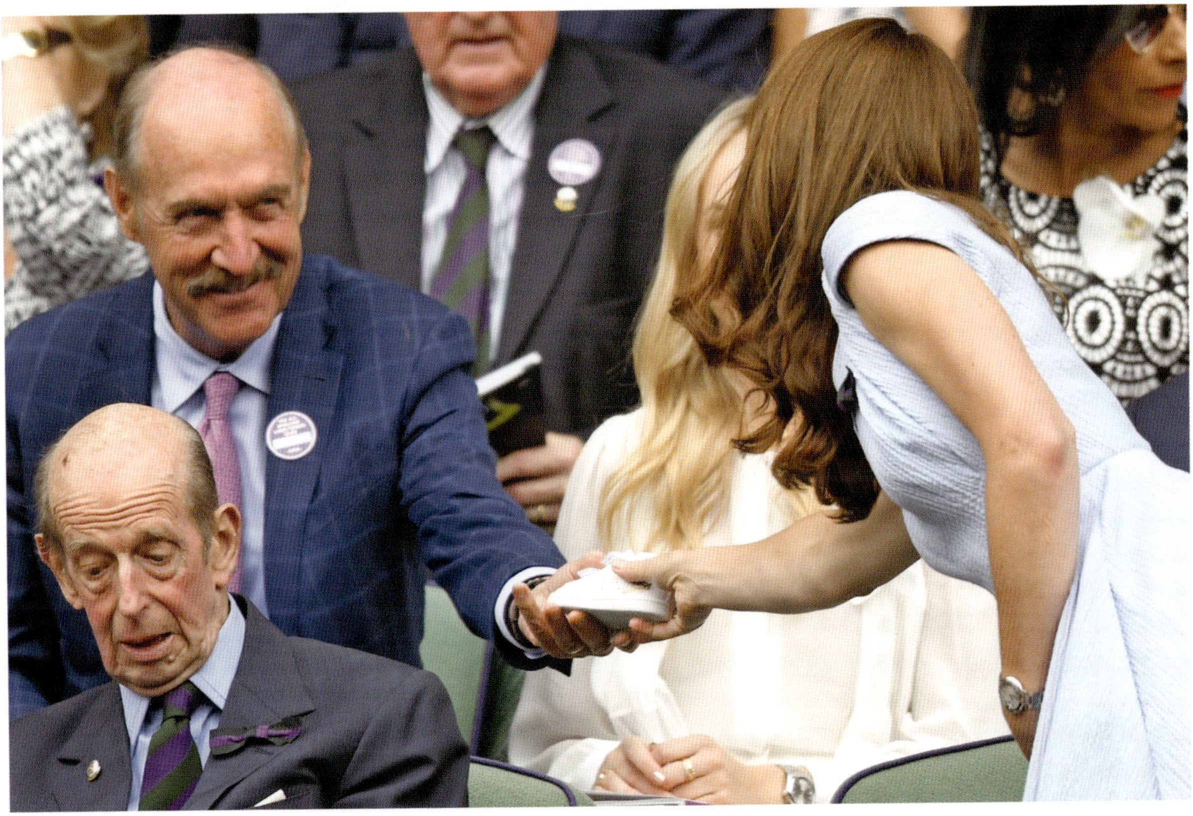

We've known Stuart Irving for years now, and he often asks us to put together events for his people, not just his valued customers. Each year his whole company votes on who demonstrates the company values best and he celebrates these achievements from staff at all levels in the organization. Our trust with one another is strong, and we've had many opportunities to serve each other. So when Stuart turned fifty, we thought about his closetful of Stan Smith Adidas shoes and decided it was time to make him a custom pair. We had them hand painted with Stuart's important life moments, the names of his children, his favorite sports team, and a celebration of his Scottish roots.

You don't have to have a pair of shoes with your face on them. It's just about getting to know people and caring about what they care about, and then when you cross paths, you re-engage by recalling those details. Maybe it takes the form of a thoughtful gift. Maybe it's remembering their favorite drink and having it waiting when they arrive. Maybe it's not just knowing their business title, but knowing how they had always hoped to take their kids out to an adventure camp in California, and so you make arrangements to help them get there.

SEND ONE TEXT OR EMAIL (RIGHT NOW, IF POSSIBLE) THAT HAS NOTHING TO DO WITH BUSINESS OR LOGISTICS, AND SIMPLY CONVEYS YOU CARE FOR SOMEONE AND WHAT'S GOING ON IN HIS OR HER LIFE.

STAN SMITH **EVENTS**

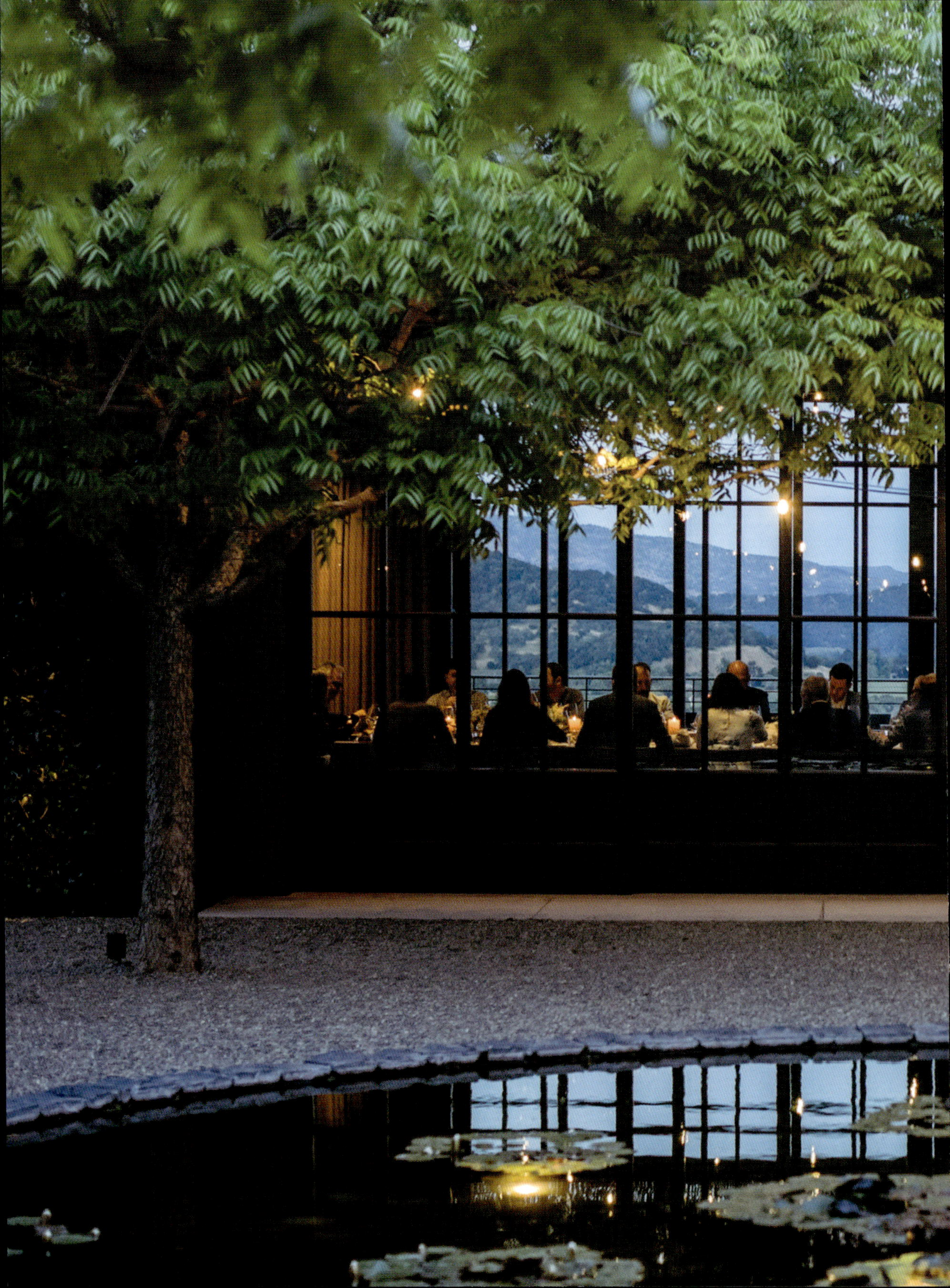

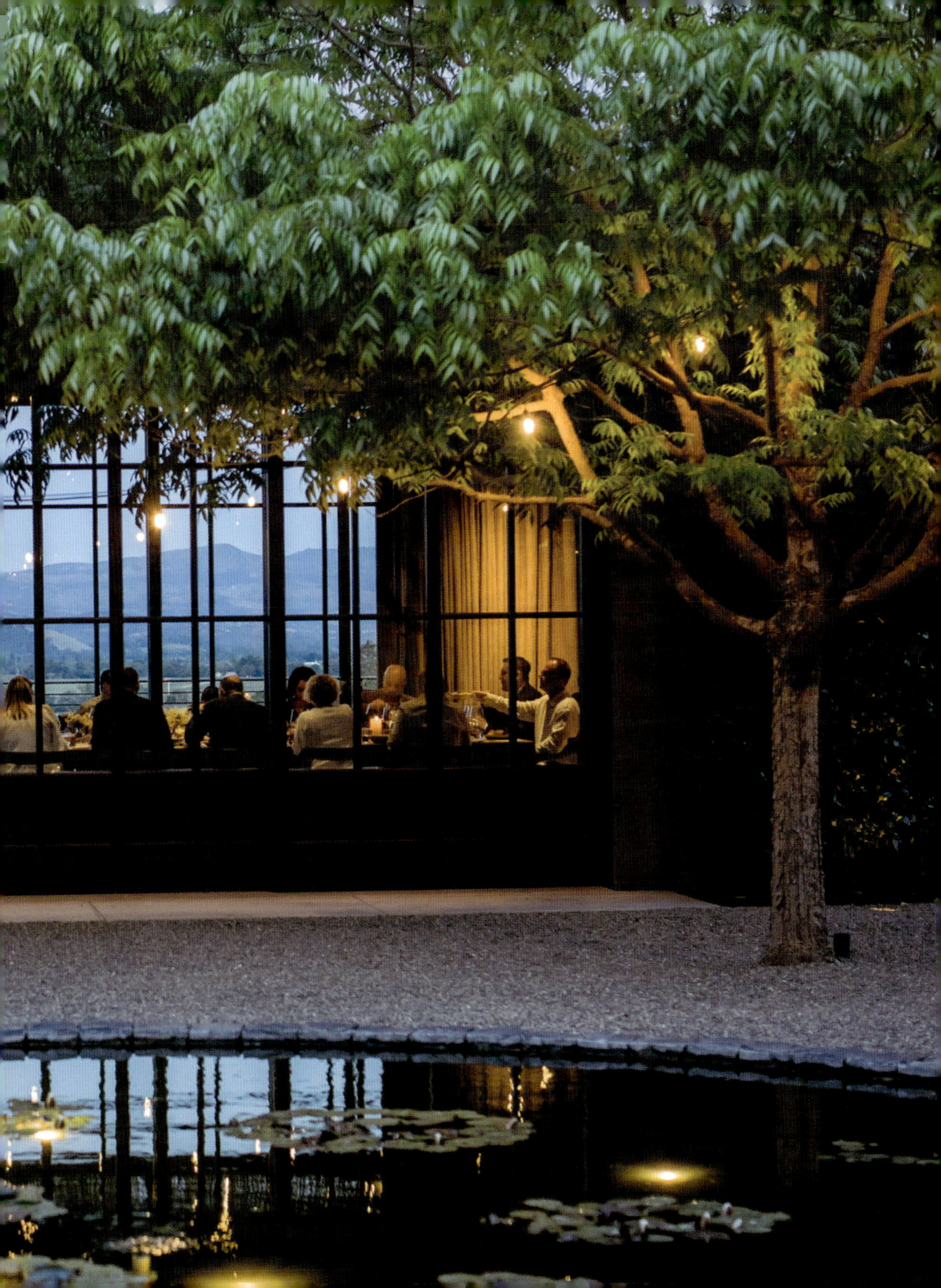

"We just started as friends who trusted each other. A few years after meeting each other, Kathy and I wanted to buy a company called Aviation Defense International—it was a British Airways security company. When we made the offer to British Airways, I told the chairman we'd save them 50 percent and get substantially higher reviews from their airport locations. We got the company. And right out of the chute we delivered on our promise—actually saving them 60 percent. Then our focus went to elevating airport reviews. When British Airways was running security, they were averaging 3s and 4s on an 8-point scale. Their highest score was a 5, and Kathy and I were determined to hit all 8s. We got there with every airport except for one, who gave us a 7. I called that location president and questioned how we fell short or what we could do to get that '8,' and she said she never gives an '8.' That's when Kathy said to call Gary. She knew he had unique access in the tennis world and had a way of making people feel really special. So I called him, and that was our first hire of Stan and Gary...and we were their first client before they were Stan Smith Events.

We got to Wimbledon with our guests, and our focus was honed in on that one customer. She brought her son with her, at Gary's suggestion for how to make it matter. We pull up to grassy courts next to Wimbledon, and there's Gary with the iconic Stan Smith and John Lloyd. Our customer and her son got to play tennis that day with legends, and the whole weekend just stayed at this high level of engagement and specialness. Gary kept introducing us to players and fascinating people, taking us into the lounges and places where the pros' families gathered. We met the Williams sisters, ate strawberries and cream, felt like VIPs.

We got the 8. From that day forward, we got it every time. Still to this day, I get notes from that customer, who has been retired now for years, telling Kathy and me that our time in Wimbledon is one of her best memories she has with her son. She is still thanking us—and we are thanking Gary and Stan.

That experience started years of working together. We hire them consistently, and they are always looking out for our best interests and making our guests feel incredibly special. It's all the little things you do in the midst of an experience that add up to something exponentially greater and bigger than how much we pay you to create an event.

I was on the elevator recently, and the VP of Global Marketing for a huge airline got on with me. We were talking about some event they were hosting, and when I asked who they hired, he said, 'We do Stan Smith Events.' I laughed and said we do too."

—FRANK ARGENBRIGHT, EXECUTIVE CHAIRMAN AND FOUNDER OF ARGENBRIGHT GROUP, FOUNDER AND CEO, SECURITY SERVICES

We didn't start our business with business. We started with friendships, getting to know people and what they were searching for, introducing them to others we thought would turn into a win-win. This had nothing to do with launching our company, because we didn't know that would even come to fruition, it was just the way we lived—and it ended up having enormous bearing on our ability to do what we felt naturally wired to do.

Our long relationship with Frank and Kathy Argenbright is really meaningful to us, and it's an example of how genuine care between people has a beautiful ripple effect over the years in many directions.

> "Before Stan Smith Events was even a thing, we brought Gary right into our family. He was coaching tennis and introducing people to one another left and right, because he's just that way. And we trusted him completely, and we knew he cared about us. I'm a very protective mother and was totally comfortable with Gary with our kids, our friends, whatever was going on."
>
> **—KATHY ARGENBRIGHT**

"Your first serve doesn't always go in. When it doesn't, you have to let it go—move on. Take the second serve. If you lose the match, move on again. Take the next opportunity to accelerate your game, to accelerate trust. Do the next good thing." —STAN SMITH

SECOND SERVES

NOTHING ABOUT BUSINESS OR LIFE IS FAIL-PROOF. In the years we've spent as professional athletes moving into the professional event space—and interacting with all sorts of high-level, dynamic, and brilliant leadership that plays at the top of the game—we know every serve won't go in. We fumble, footfault, misstep. We may make some really costly mistakes in the relationships we value most. This can be an intense and frightening spot to be in, because we don't know if we'll ever gain that trust back. The truth is, we may not. But what we can do is the "next good thing." We can own what is ours to own, apologize with transparency, and think creatively and intentionally about how to make our wrongs right. We can take a second serve.

> "A powerful thing we've witnessed is leaders who admit when they've made a mistake and lost trust—and then modeled great humility and incredible wisdom in doing what they can to rebuild trust. It isn't easy. Rebuilding trust can be harder than establishing trust in the first place. But what we've seen, heard, and experienced ourselves is that when you work to regain trust, it is often followed by an even deeper relationship." —Gary Niebur

"FIRST GO AND BE RECONCILED."
—JESUS (MATTHEW 5:24, HOLY BIBLE, NEW INTERNATIONAL VERSION)

#1 CALL OUT YOUR FAULT

Bad news gets worse the longer you wait to tell it. We've all probably seen this play out over and over in our lives, in every movie we watched as a kid, in every story of hard-won redemption. If you keep it in the dark, it gets darker. Pulling something into the light takes courage, especially when a lot is riding on the line, but in the simplest terms, if you want to build trust, tell the truth. We've told a lot of stories in this book about owning what you need to own, and this is critical in a second serve. Avoidance, faking it, blaming someone else, burying it—nothing else works, because none of those techniques honors the relationship.

> "Never delay an issue you've got to resolve because otherwise it gets worse. Own the narrative and own the solution." —RALPH ANDRETTA

"I had to pick up the phone and apologize. Right then. I had said something snarky, and it was totally the wrong thing to say, and it had the potential to make one of our biggest partners really upset. I had to own it, because I was the one who said it. So I called the other CEO and told him exactly what I said, and told him I wanted to make it up to him. And he said, 'You don't have to do anything. You showed me I'm dealing with a company that is accountable, and takes responsibility for it.' In that interaction, our trust grew. He knows I will tell him the truth." —STEVE SQUERI

#2 CHASE DOWN EVERY BALL—AGAIN

When something happens that breaks or buckles trust, we go back to the SERVE element of Elevate—chasing down every ball, every detail, and making it clear that we are giving it our all. We get back into the match with full-hearted engagement and intentionality.

"We have a foundation of trust and solidarity at Gramercy Tavern... which is also a heavy load to bear for any leader, any team. It can be damaged and lost in a short amount of time. I don't say that with panic or fear, it's more out of reverence for the act of showing up. You really do chase down every ball.

There's no such thing as a perfect game or perfect day, but our success will often be measured by how well we deal with the mistakes. And how well we read the moment and adapt. It's not over if we mess up. It's not a failure to have fallen short of someone's expectations as long as we can maintain contact with them. We hold that contact through an apology. We can assure our guest, after the apology, that we're aware we missed the mark and mean to fix it. Then we provide a creative solution, double down. If our mistake points to something in the system we need to fix, then we quickly get after that, too, so the problem doesn't get out of reach.

Some of our mistakes create the longest-lasting bonds with our guests. Some of our longest relationships actually started off with a dinner service that went wrong."—Michael Anthony

SECOND SERVES

Here's another second serve story.

We wrote about our strong friendship with Frank and Kathy Argenbright, which started before Stan Smith Events was even inked on a business card. One year, some of Kathy's acquaintances were keen to go to Roland-Garros and experience a meaningful event like they heard we were creating for others. However, in the end, they didn't want to make the financial investment to make it a more meaningful or five-star experience, so we were limited to helping secure tickets. Once they got to Roland-Garros, they regretted their choice and wished they'd chosen the full experience that they saw others having. We believed it was the right moment to chase down a ball and elevate the experience for those women with some special mementos and access to some behind-the-scenes locations. Even though we hadn't broken trust with these guests, because we delivered more than what we said we would deliver, we recognized the opportunity for a second serve. We took it, at cost to ourselves, because we care about the Argenbrights and wanted their acquaintances to feel valued in a memorable way.

We also wrote about Lena Björck earlier—someone who has done phenomenal catering work for us in the chase-down-every-ball kind of way, and who built a very successful business from the ground up. She ended up selling her business, and things went south. Her name was still on the business, and her existing clients kept using the business because she had always delivered exceptionally well. But her high-level expertise was not matched by the new leadership, and the business sank. Lena was devastated.

"I lost my confidence. I didn't have control over what the new owners were doing, but it still broke me, and I felt like a failure. I had to slowly regain confidence in other areas, and eventually found an incredible partner and we started a brand new catering company from scratch. I have a very competitive spirit, and so once I got my confidence back, I was ready to go after it. I was ready to redeem what had been lost. Because of the relationships that I had built with amazing clients in all the years prior, and because of the grace they were willing to give me, I'm back on my feet."

—LENA BJÖRCK, OWNER IN THE RESTAURANT AND HOSPITALITY INDUSTRY, FORMER BUSINESSWOMAN OF THE YEAR IN THE UK

#3 CREATE NEW MOMENTS THAT MATTER

We've talked throughout this book about how to accelerate trust in your key relationships. Second serve moments might be the moments that matter the most, because they are also likely the last chance we'll get in that relationship.

> "It's a lot harder to regain trust than to gain it the first time. The effort level is exponential." —KEVIN WARREN

> "If we didn't have the relational equity, we wouldn't receive a second chance."
> —DANIELLE VINCENT

As you think about taking a second SERVE, flip back through this playbook. Revisit strategy and how you'll get to that hook your (now) skeptical guest will say "yes" to. Think about how you can engage with that person or group in very honest, transparent ways—which likely includes opening up about the mistake, owning it, and volleying toward a new solution that honors them. Get around a table for a family-style meal. Bring some lightheartedness into the moment, and breathing space, rather than making it all about business or the problem at hand. Surprise and delight along the way, maybe with a special memento, something unique they love, or something that points to you remembering a detail about their life that's significant and will help them feel seen, known, and valued.

It's possible that a second serve will create an even stronger bond. It's also possible, of course, that it won't produce the results you hoped. But take a long view. Be patient, transparent, and engaged. Think outside the box and woo your relationship back into good standing.

> "Trust isn't a one time thing. There are opportunities every day to keep applying your SERVE." —GARY NIEBUR

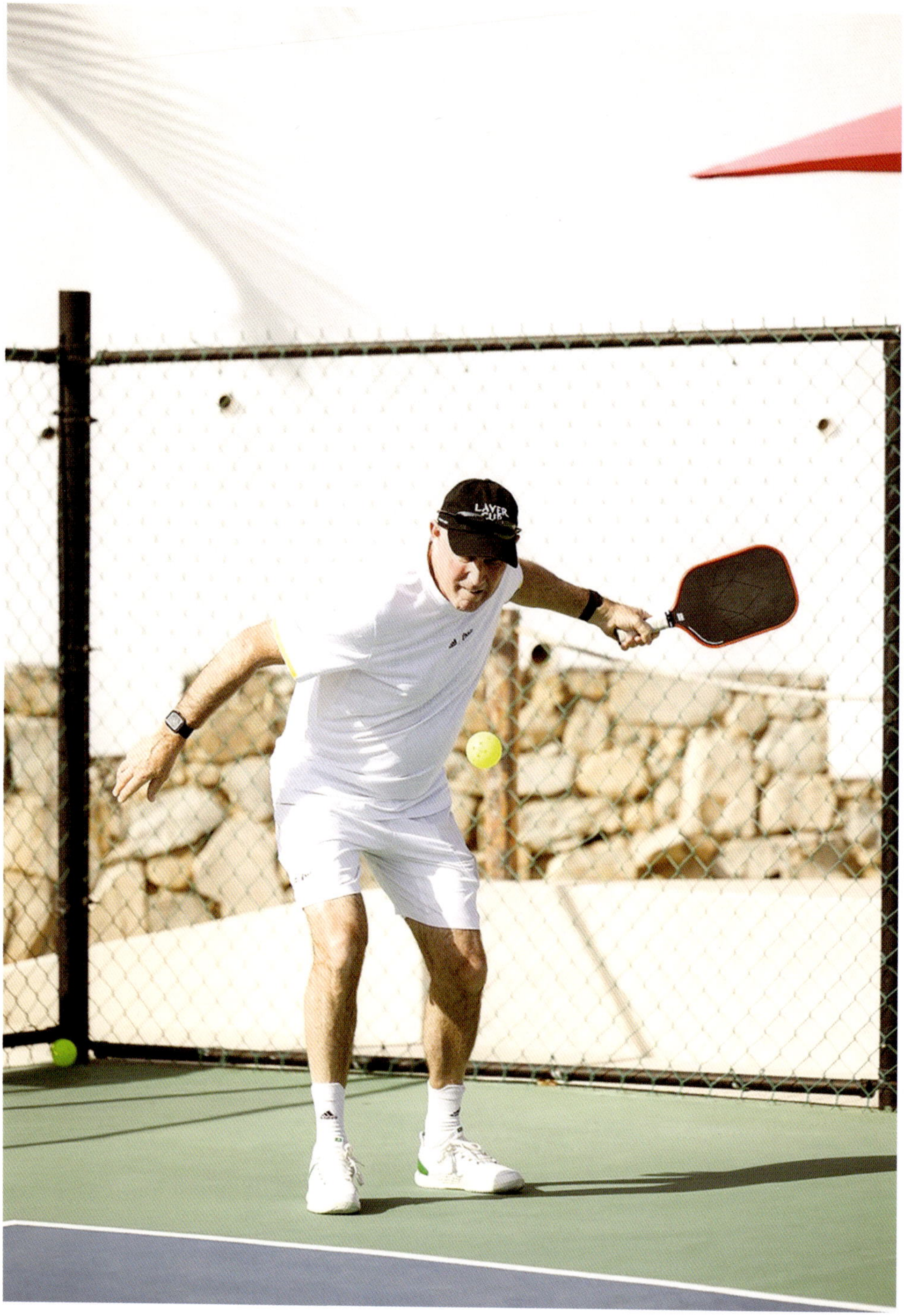

TRY YOUR SERVE

THIS IS THE PLACE TO DIG INTO WHAT *SERVE* **CAN LOOK LIKE** for your own valued business and life relationships. Maybe you've already responded to prompts in earlier chapters, so flip to wherever you've kept notes to refresh your memory. Then grab a pen. Get a trusted teammate if it makes sense to do so. And let's start walking through some simple steps to make SERVE actionable and concrete.

DOWNLOAD A PDF COPY OF THE
TRY YOUR SERVE WORKBOOK SECTION
BY SCANNING THIS QR CODE.

TRY YOUR SERVE

THIS IS YOUR PLAYBOOK

PART ONE

1: LIST YOUR KEY RELATIONSHIPS (WORK AND PERSONAL).

2: LIST THE PEOPLE YOU DON'T YET HAVE A RELATIONSHIP WITH, BUT WHO YOU FEEL IT'S IMPORTANT TO DEVELOP A RELATIONSHIP WITH.

3: FROM THOSE LISTS, CIRCLE THE NAMES OF THOSE WITH WHOM YOU MOST NEED TO DEEPEN TRUST.

4: NOW, TAKE A FEW MINUTES AND THINK ABOUT THESE RELATIONSHIPS. STAR ONE FROM YOUR WORK LIFE; THEN STAR ONE FROM YOUR PERSONAL LIFE. (IF YOU'RE GETTING STUCK, FLIP BACK THROUGH THIS BOOK AND ANY RESPONSES YOU WROTE IN THE MARGINS, OR ANYTHING YOU UNDERLINED...AND CONSIDER WHO THAT MAY APPLY TO.)

TRY YOUR SERVE

PART TWO

WORK RELATIONSHIP I'M GOING TO *SERVE*:

PERSONAL RELATIONSHIP I'M GOING TO *SERVE*:

PART THREE

HERE'S WHERE WE DIG INTO EACH *SERVE* ELEMENT FOR WHERE YOU WANT TO CREATE A MOMENT THAT MATTERS. SOME MAY COME MORE EASILY THAN OTHERS, BUT PUT THE MOST AMOUNT OF TIME INTO THE FIRST ONE: THE "S." AND IF IT HELPS, FLIP BACK THROUGH THE STRATEGIZE CHAPTER TO REVISIT THOSE PLANNING TIPS.

WORK RELATIONSHIP:

S

E

R

V

E

TRY YOUR SERVE

PERSONAL RELATIONSHIP:

S

E

R

V

E

Strategize: design moments that matter
Use your team and resources to plan a unique, delightful atmosphere that opens up the opportunity to win trust in important relationships.

Engage: open hearts
Care about and engage with the whole person—not just the transaction or business deal—so each client and guest feels known, valued, and comfortable in any given situation.

Recreate: play together
Build bonds and shared memories through fun experiences like team challenges and mini tournaments. Guards come down; trust grows.

Volley: rally your way forward
Problem-solve with direction and optimism—letting ideas flow without defensiveness or ego—so the end result both solidifies trust and innovates into new spaces.

Elevate: chase down every ball
Nail every detail so the entire experience exceeds expectations with special invitations, unique access, customized gifts, or surprise moments that solidify a trusted relationship.

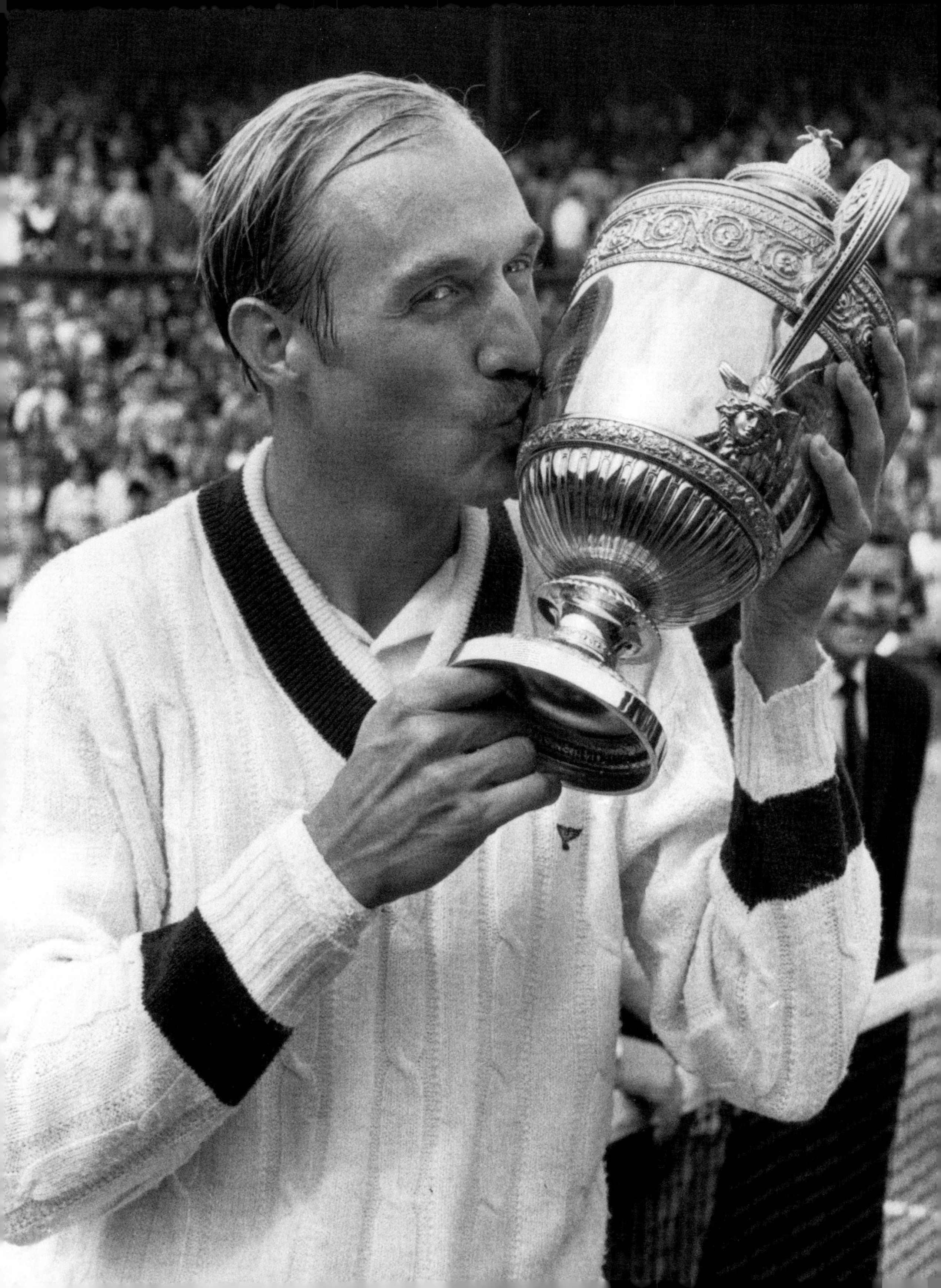

PART FOUR
RELATIONSHIP #1:

NOW THAT YOU HAVE YOUR *SERVE* OUTLINED, DECIDE WHEN THIS MOMENT THAT MATTERS WILL HAPPEN.

DATE:

PERSON:

WHAT OTHER PEOPLE DO YOU NEED TO LEAN INTO, TO PULL THIS OFF?

NEXT TO EACH NAME, WRITE WHAT PART THEY WILL PLAY. REACH OUT TO EACH PERSON ON YOUR LIST, AS SOON AS POSSIBLE.

TRY YOUR SERVE

RELATIONSHIP #2:

DATE:	PERSON:
WHAT OTHER PEOPLE DO YOU NEED TO LEAN INTO, TO PULL THIS OFF?	NEXT TO EACH NAME, WRITE WHAT PART THEY WILL PLAY. REACH OUT TO EACH PERSON ON YOUR LIST, AS SOON AS POSSIBLE.

TRY YOUR SERVE

PART FIVE
RELATIONSHIP #1:

BEGIN TO EXECUTE YOUR *SERVE*. PURCHASE OR BORROW THE THINGS YOU NEED. RESERVE THE SPOTS. CALL IN FAVORS TO GET ACCESS. IF YOU HIT A ROADBLOCK, RE-IMAGINE AND VOLLEY YOUR WAY INTO A NEW SOLUTION WITH OPTIMISM AND SELF-CONTROL. (ASK A CREATIVE OR NETWORKED FRIEND IF YOU'RE REALLY STUCK.)

NOTES

TRY YOUR SERVE

RELATIONSHIP #2:

BEGIN TO EXECUTE YOUR *SERVE*. PURCHASE OR BORROW THE THINGS YOU NEED. RESERVE THE SPOTS. CALL IN FAVORS TO GET ACCESS. IF YOU HIT A ROADBLOCK, RE-IMAGINE AND VOLLEY YOUR WAY INTO A NEW SOLUTION WITH OPTIMISM AND SELF-CONTROL. (ASK A CREATIVE OR NETWORKED FRIEND IF YOU'RE REALLY STUCK.)

NOTES

PART SIX

Above all else, remember why you're doing this: because people matter most. Take good care of them. Invest and bond. Let's create moments that matter...so they do.

TRY YOUR SERVE

NOTES

ACKNOWLEDGMENTS

TO LIZ BELL YOUNG FOR BEING THE PERFECT FIT TO COME ALONGSIDE US IN WRITING THIS BOOK. WE ARE FOREVER GRATEFUL FOR YOUR CARE, GUIDANCE, AND CREATIVE DIRECTION THROUGHOUT THE ENTIRE PROCESS.

TO JONATHAN BOLDEN FOR YOUR WISDOM, ENCOURAGEMENT, AND INPUT, WHICH WAS KEY IN NARROWING THE FOCUS FOR THIS BOOK AND FOR WHAT'S NEXT FOR STAN SMITH EVENTS.

TO DAVID VALENTINE FOR INVESTING YOUR TALENTS IN THE BRANDING AND DESIGN

TO MARY MORGAN HEAD FOR ALL YOUR ORGANIZATIONAL SUPPORT AND INSIGHT THROUGHOUT THE PROCESS

TO KOBUS JOHNSEN FOR PUBLISHING AND DOING MORE THAN WE COULD HAVE IMAGINED

TO BEN ORTLIP FOR HELPING US GET STARTED AND PROVIDING GREAT GUIDANCE

TO JIM LEVINE FOR COACHING US THROUGH THE EARLY STAGES OF THE WRITING AND PUBLISHING PROCESS

TO DANNY MEYER FOR YOUR FRIENDSHIP AND PARTNERSHIP

TO BOB LEWIS FOR BEING A GREAT LEADERSHIP COACH

TO DON BAER FOR YOUR CONTRIBUTIONS AT THE BEGINNING OF OUR TRUST JOURNEY

TO DAVE HILL FOR YOUR MENTORSHIP

TO DAVID SALYERS FOR BEING A REMARKABLE SOUNDING BOARD

TO HAP KLOPP FOR YOUR WISDOM AND INSIGHT

TO DAN MOHAN FOR YOUR COUNSEL

TO ALL THE AMAZING PHOTOGRAPHERS WHO HAVE CAPTURED OUR EVENTS AROUND THE WORLD

TO ALL THE TALENT INCLUDING ATHLETES, ACTORS, CHEFS, AND SOMMELIERS FOR ENGAGING AND RECREATING SO WELL OVER THE YEARS

TO OUR REMARKABLE VENDORS FOR MODELING SERVE ALONGSIDE US

TO OUR LOYAL CLIENTS FOR TRUSTING US

TO OUR DEVOTED TEAM AT STAN SMITH EVENTS FOR HELPING US BRING SERVE TO LIFE

PHOTOGRAPHY CREDITS

ANNA GODWIN, PAGE 35

CHRISTY USHER, CHRISTINE ROBIN PHOTOGRAPHY, PAGE 33

DAMION HAMILTON, PAGES 108, 182

DANI WILKERSON – SOUTHWEST AIRLINES, PAGE 111

DANIEL JIREH, PAGES 50, 198

DANIEL KRIEGER, PAGE 8

DAVID VALENTINE, PAGE 181

DENIS REGGIE, PAGES 19, 21, 40

ESTHER HONG, PAGES 55, 109, 113, 143

EXPLORE GROUP NEW ZEALAND, PAGES 112, 124

FRANCESCO SAPIENZA, PAGE 169

FRED MULLANE/CAMERAWORK USA, PAGE 7, 13, 15, 47, 81, 87, 95, 179, 195

GEORGES VUONG, PAGE 164

GETTY IMAGES, PAGES 60, 154, 172, 179, 205

IVANA MICIC, PAGES 4, 16, 50 ,175

JH AOTEAROA, PAGE 114

KANE JARROD, PAGES 46, 105, 140, 164

KELLI WHITE, PAGES 52, 112

LINDSAY ERNST, PAGES 16, 147, 160, 193

MIKE RITTERBECK, PAGES 70, 74, 105, 136, 177

PETER VAN DEN BERG, PAGE 22

RICHARD CASHIN, PAGES 101, 104, 119

SCOTT GIBSON, PAGE 25

SCOTT WILSON, PAGE 148

SHERMAN CHU PHOTOGRAPHER, PAGES 10, 29, 39, 78, 104, 119, 139, 114

STAN SMITH ARCHIVES, PAGES 15, 36, 45, 50, 56, 77, 80, 81, 88, 91, 107, 109, 153, 161, 163, 165,167, 181

STEVEN MORRIS, PAGES 17, 123, 150

UNINTERRUPTED, PAGE 63